2016

Sarah Hesketh is a writer and editor from Pendle, in East ~~~~
She is the author of the poetry collections *Napoleon's Travelling Bookshelf* (Penned in the Margins, 2009) and *The Hard Word Box* (Penned in the Margins, 2014), and the editor of *The Emma Press Anthology of Age* (2015). She has been an Artist in Residence with Age Concern and The Holocaust Memorial Day Trust. Her work has a focus on socially engaged writing practices and in 2022 she was awarded a Royal Society of Literature 'Literature Matters' Award. She currently lives in London and works as Managing Editor for *Modern Poetry in Translation*.

2016

Sarah Hesketh

CB editions

First published in Great Britain in 2025
by CB editions
146 Percy Road London W12 9QL
www.cbeditions.com

SC&JL

Cover photo by Jimmy Symonds (jimmysymonds.com)

Printed and bound in the UK by CMP Books

ISBN 978-1-7394212-5-0

There are things
We live among 'and to see them
Is to know ourselves'.

. . . .

But I will listen to a man, I will listen to a man, and when I
speak I will speak, tho he will fail and I will fail. But I will
listen to him speak.

– George Oppen, *Of Being Numerous*

'we are far more united and have far more in common
with each other than things that divide us'

– Jo Cox, MP

Preface

It is difficult
to get the news from poems
yet men die miserably every day
for lack
of what is found there

– William Carlos Williams, 'Asphodel, That Greeny Flower'

'Shitshow', 'trashcan fire', 'the worst year ever' – the end-of-the-year round-ups for the year 2016 were not kind. Politics had gone crazy, in many remarkable ways. UK and American society seemed to be in an irretrievable process of fragmentation and polarisation. A lot of people died, including my own father.

They say that in the six months after a major loss you shouldn't make any big life decisions. Two weeks after my father died I applied for a PhD scholarship at the University of Roehampton focusing on the use of interview transcripts in poetic practice. At the end of September, I was informed that I had been lucky enough to be selected for the scholarship. In January 2017 I had to choose a topic for my new writing project. Donald Trump was about to be inaugurated as the 45th President of the USA. Western society felt to be buckling under the weight of (sur)reality – and in the words of the great American poet C. D. Wright, 'I wanted to see if my art could handle that hoe' (*One Big Self*, Copper Canyon Press, 2003).

This book is an attempt at a reckoning with a particular point in history, from my own particular view of the stage. It is not a comprehensive work of history. But through the voiced experiences of real people who lived through this tumultuous time, it explores twelve key public events that occurred in 2016: the UK Brexit vote, the election of Donald Trump, the Syrian refugee crisis, the murder of UK MP Jo Cox, the death of David Bowie, the death of Carrie Fisher, British

Home Stores going into administration, the re-election of Jeremy Corbyn as Labour Party leader, Leicester City's fairy-tale triumph in the Premier League, and the growing climate crisis as 2016 recorded the hottest global temperature rises since records began (these records have since been exceeded).

The book began as twelve interviews with twelve different individuals. After conducting these interviews I transcribed them in full. The resulting manuscript was then composed through a process of editing and collage. All these words were spoken, but not necessarily in this order. Human speech is, like any other text, a highly creative genre. As Nobel Laureate Svetlana Alexievich says of her own use of transcripts as a literary form: 'I compose not reality (because to grasp reality is impossible), but its image; an image of our time; the way we see it and the way we represent it to ourselves.' ('Through the Eyes of a Humanist: The Polyphonic Realities of Svetlana Alexievich', *Overland* 226, August 2017).

The book follows a thematic structure that explores issues of race, feminism, immigration, the role of the media, how we choose our heroes and how we can creatively respond to times of crisis. It has moments of darkness – discussing Jo Cox's death and the situation in the Moria refugee camp. It also has moments of great humour as the speakers undercut their own thoughts and experiences. It demonstrates that people are complicated – even when we profess to hold particular views or beliefs, we are often inconsistent. The book is an attempt to find hope in the act of conversation, to demonstrate that even in the midst of incredible violence and disagreement, when our words are placed side by side on the page it can be seen that we are, as Jo Cox MP put it in her maiden speech to the House of Commons, 'far more united and have far more in common with each other than things that divide us'.

The manuscript was largely composed between 2017 and 2020. Reading it as we approach the tenth anniversary of these events, it is interesting to question whether the narrative of hope, of faith in human potential that I built into the structure of this text, is justified, or if we remain stagnated and polarised. Personally, I choose to adopt the position of David Buckland, one of the interviewees, when he says:

> i mean, it
> doesn't matter two beans to anybody or
> history whether i am optimistic or pessimistic,
> so i'd much rather choose to be optimistic

This book has many authors and I am incredibly grateful and for-ever indebted to all of the interviewees who chose to put their trust in me and contribute to the project. Some have chosen to remain anony-mous. I am eternally grateful to them for gifting me their words. To those who have chosen to be identified – Ghias Aljundi, Grant Atter-bury, David Buckland, Michael Drucquer, Sally Ann Fitt and Steph-anie Smith – the same huge thank-you for your ongoing generosity and support.

People are brilliant. Human life as it is lived on a daily basis is hard and fascinating and beautiful and sad and funny. It can be hard to remember that, whatever socio-political-historic moment we are navi-gating in the present.

And as one voice in the book says, it's not

> let's just all come together 'kum ba
> ya.' no, not at all. we have to fight
> for what we believe in. and you
> know, put your case. and let's work
> with as many people as possible to
> do that

2016 is a very small, but hopefully enjoyable, contribution to that work.

listen

the first rough draft   of history   is speaking

old men wishing   to drool about their youth
the past   marching by in smart review
    rewritten
to the point of feeling
        the shirt sleeved
multitudes are   scrubbing up their truths

for you they'll plumb this curious timestamp   perhaps

tongue a story or two

well the first thing i want to say, it's interesting because it's a little bit about you as well, it's interesting that you said your dad died, sorry. i'm sorry to hear that. but you said that it was afterwards that you kind of decided to do this   also you said something about   i can't remember what you said. and obviously i'm not trying to compare the loss of a stranger to the loss of a father. i lost my father twenty years ago   it was absolutely devastating. twenty-one years ago   but, it's funny how any loss reminds you of other losses. er, and then also i can't remember what you said that reminded me of this but after a terrible loss, like of my father, which was awful. one of the things is you sort of, you have a 'don't-give-a-shitness' afterwards. i can remember saying a couple of things to people who i hadn't   who needed things saying to them. it's like – no, not allowed. actually – you, you're behaving badly. and i think it's shit. which i wouldn't have been brave enough to say before. something like that. and there's a kind of, you know, liberation that you give yourself after a loss.   because that's what it's all about. it's life and death is the fucking ultimate thing! and you, you don't want to try and pass onto anybody really what it's like and you can't, really. until you've actually had that wrench and that confusion and how can it be true that it's still – that the trees are still upright? you know, i remember when my father died, seeing in all the poems and everything, seeing, 'the trees bend over at the top' and thinking, but, but, but, but, it's not! they don't give a shit! everything's the same. everything's the same and yet my world is utterly upside down. it's really an extraordinary thing

well funnily enough i can, i was four, which was the moon landing. the moon landing i remember very very well because my mum was very excited about it and got us out of bed
        i mean to me, it was in the middle of the night. i don't know, maybe it was at 8 o'clock in the evening, i really don't know. but when the moon landing happened she got us out of bed. and we watched it, and of course Space Oddity was played a lot at that time. i would be lying if i said i've got an actual memory of listening to Space Oddity, but, but that is the truth. that i would have heard that and that was playing a lot on the telly. oh my god, what's this? we're allowed to come out of the bedroom? and sit there with my sister. and you know, look out at the moon. i do remember there being this sound. so the whole atmosphere of it. i'm a very audial person. i sing. i think that i process things very audially. and i find that in lots of ways   evidence for that and   not being able to switch off when someone's talking, and other people can just let it go over their head and i can't. eurrgh! and like a jingle or whatever, earworms. i just absorb sound a lot. so i do remember: atmosphere, sound and, you know, vision!
        then there's another bit of confusion – you don't know whether it's false memory or not. because. and, and like neuro-scientifically, isn't it that all memories are recreated every time, kind of thing, so sometimes you just don't know

George Michael dying, because i remember
bursting into tears. that was Boxing Day. it was
just the end of a really long cycle. you know
it wasn't him   the fact that it was another
one. it was just, no! not another one. it was just
too much. i think it was for everybody that was
sort of my age. i think it brought us   it
brought it all up to us that everybody we'd
grown up with and fallen in love with was
gonna die   and it wasn't going to get any
better. it was a harsh year because a lot of
people went. but then you kind of realise
this is the point   because we grew up in a
television age, people older than us   they
didn't watch them on their TV every day. they
didn't see them on chat. they didn't have
photos. every year now, more and more people
are going to die. and we're going to lose them,
and we maybe at some point we'll get inured to
it, and we won't feel it anymore. but 2016
seemed to be a year when we went, oh, this is
what's gonna happen. we're gonna lose Bowie
        every year there's gonna be that because of
course everybody's gonna   but we know
them so much better than they did

i one day was watching the news on the Newsnight on the second of October 2015. and, there was a piece of news about a boat sank in the Mediterranean. i couldn't follow the news any more. and i said to my partner, i'm going tomorrow. yeah. i went. i just grabbed my laptop, booked a ticket, blindly

one night to arrange things: to find a place, to find where to go, where the boats were coming. and, i flew in the morning directly to Lesvos. i remember when arriving, it's mostly the boats coming on a place called 'dirt road'. it's like one of the most beautiful places in Lesvos, maybe, but it's a dirt road. like rocks and stones and if you take a car there it's very likely to break down after two weeks. we were driving in the taxi from the arrival and a boat came

i said, 'i'm out.' left my bag – he could've taken everything – left my bag, my laptop, my everything, and went into the water. that was the first   the idea came in one second, and the first boat came in one second, too. no plan

i had the overwhelming feeling that i just want to save these guys. i wasn't scared at all. i grew by the sea in Syria. i'm not scared of the water at all. but   the encounter wasn't a scary feeling, but it was a special, weird, strange, warm, all these contradictions in one thing. in one package. i went out with my trousers on, i had water up to here. so my wallet, my mobile, everything was under water. i started from there. my ticket was for one week, so i was supposed to go back home on the tenth of October. and i kept missing that flight. i came back to London on the twenty-eighth. i went, and for the next twelve months i didn't miss any month. i went once every month until April – then i stayed eight weeks in one go

i started going, actually, to watch football
i just
wanted to see football. i was working very
hard. i often went on my own. and i just
wanted to see a football match   then
somebody from Notts County. Notts County
were playing Leicester and they, he, took a big
group of us up to see them, on a bit of a jolly
and i was
surrounded by these people, we were in the
Notts County supporters' area and they were
playing Leicester. and, Leicester appealed a
penalty, which i thought was a barn-door
penalty. and i stood up, and shouted at the
referee: 'ref, come on! it's a penalty!' and that's
when i suddenly realised, i've become a
Leicester City supporter. i must have done.
you know
here i am standing up
shouting. i'd got sucked in! i'd got sucked in.
you know, by going to see them. and by the
ethos of the club. the atmosphere, and the
history of them, everything. and you start to
get to know the players, you start to follow
them. you start to take an interest and there
you are − you suddenly find yourself a
supporter

i came completely out of artistic enquiry

a funny little piece of information about these scientists had mapped the whole of the North Atlantic Ocean. now, i'm a sailor, and i know how complicated oceans are and i thought, well, that's crazy. you can't digitally map something that complex. this was in '98   so, when i got back to England i was curious   and what this guy Richard Wood, a mathematician, had done, was manage to make the first big climate model   the only, the first time humanity, human beings had a tool like this. and it fascinated me as an artist. because artists always dream of the future. we always speculate and construct the future. here was a mathematician saying, it is very likely, in ten years' time this will happen. fifteen years, twenty years   what he had was the data from two hundred years ago. so he set his model running two hundred years ago, followed it through to the present, and it was actually incredibly accurate and   quite alarming what he was saying. so he then said, well, you should go and talk to the oceanographers. so this is all me being artistically curious these oceanographers, were the ones who were kind of gathering the data that fed the information into his mathematical model. and i was just deadly curious about it all. and then they came back and said, look, why is nobody listening to us? we have this really urgent piece of information about climate change.   i thought, well, you know, the problem is, their language is, you know, you can't decipher it. i would like to take a scientist to bed with me, in that sense that i take Ian McEwan. impossible! so i thought well, ok, could we somehow set up a language that wasn't scientific, but said the same thing. so, the whole idea, of me going up to the Arctic on a sailing boat with scientists and artists, was to somehow try and get these   brains to come up with a different way of talking about climate change   cultural challenge rather than a scientific challenge. so that was kind of how it all came about. which was, you know, that was me being an artist so i joined specifically to vote for Jeremy Corbyn in the leadership contest. i think an older woman at work actually said to me, when we were on a night out and everyone was arguing about politics   she was like, are you a paid-up member of the Labour party then? and i was like, no. and she was like, well what are you talking about then? if you're not even a member then why are you arguing with me, and i thought, well, that's true. i kept thinking about it. and i remember you had to pay thirty pounds. and it was the day before payday. literally the day before, and there was this girl at work who also   joined to vote for him. and she was like, i'll lend you the money so you can join, and we can vote for him   so it was we all felt like we were in it together   because i felt like. for the first time, i was like, what we're all talking about and doing, could make a difference. which, especially with voting, when, i remember my mum saying oh, you have to be careful, because, erm, you, sometimes it might be better to vote for the Libdems in your area because it'll stop the Tories getting in. and it just all felt a bit like, so, not – so your vote doesn't really matter. you have to be strategic. whereas this was like, no, i want Jeremy Corbyn to be leader of the Labour party. and i want to support him. and i want to do that, rather than just trying to stop the Tories from getting in most of the conversations have been shrouded in sound bites, in, you know. recycled commentary. and, and bollocks, basically. but i've always, sort of. i think it's important to reflect, and see what the, if there are any disparities between my reasons for voting Leave, then, and – now. if you see what i mean. and, to see how much truth there is   it's, it's, it's all recycled, selective facts, soundbites and stuff. and actually, if you drill down into people's real reasons for voting either way

really explore that, i think it's quite interesting   my politics are that, i'm, i suppose. i have some quite left-wing views – animal rights, and stuff like that. i mean i think you should get life in prison if you, you know, don't feed your cat. you know what i mean? i'm, i'm, huge, huge on animal rights, for example. minimum wage, you know. i don't like any form of exploitation. but i suppose, you know, if, when i do all the sort of political tests, or whatever, i suppose i am centre-right. but i'm not a traditional conservative. i'm a working-class, from a council house, alright a very nice council house, but i'm from council housing. and, i don't believe in privatisation, i despise toffs and people that went to Oxbridge and whatever. i don't like it when people pigeonhole me as, oh, you know you're a Tory. i'm not a Tory. i have voted Conservative. and i do vote Conservative. but i'm not a 'Tory', if that makes sense?

when i was, 24, i got my first job as an assistant
to a member of the European Parliament, a Labour
MEP. and Jo was down the corridor, an assistant to
Glenys Kinnock, MEP. Glenys was like, well known
as being like, really – always employed amazing
assistants. and Jo was a couple of years older than
me. so it was a bit like when you're at school and if
you're in fifth year, the person in upper sixth is like,
a lot older. so she was one of the gold standard, like,
'oh *Jo*.' Jo Leadbetter as she was then. and, we just
had riotous laughs in our twenties, yeah, just
normal, over-drinking, out partying. some political
chat, but more focus on, you know, what
twentysomethings are usually bothered about
then into our thirties and then, we did something
that was quite exciting. we, we were at Labour Party
Conference, there we were, these two kind of,
northern Yorkshire girl – women, i guess, not girls.
there was probably going to be an election the next
year. and she said, 'have you ever thought about
becoming an MP?' i said, well, i've sort of thought
about it but, you know, i'd be really embarrassed i'd
be a bit shit. and she was like, 'oh we should do like,
training'. i was like, yeah. 'shall we go and find out
about the training?' the last day of conference
Labour Women's Network, they were just actually
packing up the stall. and she was like, 'you go.' and
i said, 'no, you go, you go.' and i sort of, slightly hid
behind her. which was a bit difficult because, i'm,
about eight inches taller than her. and er, she said,
'hi, i'm just enquiring about er, these training
courses.' they said, 'well, we've got one coming up
in a couple of weeks. do you want to do it? it's in
Newcastle on the weekend.' we're like, yeah, go on
then. and yeah, we went, and we just had a brilliant
time on this course

and it just makes me – all politics is so horrifying. including on my side. i get horrified at what people do. we cast a furtive glance at what our own people do, so. i dunno. i had to vote for someone so Trump got the job   trust me when i say the Republicans do things that drive me crazy, also. yes, ma'am. i think we are way too, as a party, we are way too, way way way too beholden to big oil. i think it's insane   they can belch smoke into our air   you know politics is just a nasty business and, and, and what i am consistently forced to do is to, if, one has any kind of moral compass, is to say – which one of these *horrible* options is the least one you know, it's rare, rare indeed to have someone where you can give a full-throated endorsement and say, this person is one hundred percent in line with what i believe. those people will not be elected. someone who believes what i believe, and says what i say, and thinks what i think, that person has a zero chance of being elected in a secular society   hopefully i am consistent, in that, i am for all life. um, [*pause*] not, not to the point where the person has no say in it, towards the end of life. it just. i think everybody ought to be given a chance! it's such a wonderful world. i don't know why – we can discuss this all day, but that did play into it for sure so you just – what do i do here?   the idea is not to have a four-year king – the thing is to hire someone to do a job. and if i was a business owner – and i am partial owner in the business that is the United States of America, i need someone who is going to do the best job. so the person that i hired with my vote, and my tax dollars, is Donald Trump. and, if i owned a company and somebody was a, at least in his past, a misogynistic bozo, but could be relied upon to do a terrific job. that's actually part of conservatism to   say look, can you do the job?

it was   obvious there was no investment in the store. stuff like the penny-pinching with our shifts and our wages and all that sort of stuff. the store, the lift was constantly breaking down and they would get someone to sort of like, bodge it up never, they would never sort of fork out any money for actual proper repairs or anything. and er, then obviously there was the bombshell of the pound sale that didn't seem a particularly promising sign. [*laughs*] i remember, er, i mean that was quite a funny time. i was   checking on my phone because i'd heard rumours it was going to happen. so, i went around as soon as it happened, i was sort of showing everyone and telling everyone. i actually got told off by the boss   as i said, the managers, not always the brightest people. he sort of came barging down and said, 'i'll thank you not to tell my staff we've been sold for a pound. if we are sold, it'll be more like a billion pounds.' in that sort of like way, that 'my dad's bigger than your dad.' so i just sort of whipped my phone out and showed him the BBC news item. he went a bit quiet   i think, i think people had massive faith. because it had been there so long. it was sort of, like almost everyone there. you know, their grandparents had been. i mean, my grandparents used to shop there, you know what i mean? it just felt like,

it was kind of hard to comprehend that it could go   that it could go that quick. it was like a kind of, British institution   before they found out it had gone for a pound – which is not a promising sign, even if you're not a business expert. you know if the company you work for is currently valued at a pound – which is what happened with Homebase a few months back – i think i've cursed everywhere i go. it suddenly gets sold for a pound. apparently i devalue firms massively, when i turn up to work there. but, yeah   we were just sort of constantly told at all times, you know, keep calm and carry on, what have you. and 'everything was fine, we had a great bunch of investors, and er, it had never been a more exciting time to work for BHS' which, in a sense, was true

i wrote something after the 2015 election saying, 'is Cameron Houdini or a Rogue Trader?' and now we know. it was clear to me   once we made the mistake of actually winning that general election, it was clear it was going to happen   it was in our election manifesto, so we had promised it. and we made lots of promises in that manifesto that were supposed to be discarded in the coalition negotiations. suddenly this stuff had to be done.   similar examples were, you know, the reduction in housing benefit and other things that became very unpopular   i wanted to re-elect the coalition   as it became clear that we were going to get a majority rather than a minority government, i started to realise we were going to have to have this Europe referendum now
but the big mistake i made in Brexit predictions was to think that Theresa May was going to bring the country together, have a moderate Brexit of some kind, keep our cabinet together, and negotiate things. and   i was wrong. it seems even the cabinet were wrong and weren't told about her   position until the 'citizens of nowhere' speech. it was a horrible speech. it was a Viktor Orbán type speech. she's   very keen on redistributing wealth, promoting public services. very keen on racial equality. she did an awful lot to promote women in the party. but she ended up with this quasi-fascist speech

so, i thought it was. i thought
it was a joke. because i was, i
don't know, i feel like the race
seemed like it was gonna be
really boring   one
of my colleagues was, like, it's
going to be a really depressing
election.   it's   gonna   be,
another Bush vs Clinton race.
and we're like, whatever. and
then   Donald   Trump
announced his candidacy, it
was like, what the fuck? and
then, this guy's not actually
going to run. he's not serious.
he's not going to make it. and
then – famous last words

i mean, we're not advocating, we're not. you know, we don't petition governments to change.   artists don't get in that territory. i mean the lobbying is done by Greenpeace and other folk, which is great. but it's not what artists do   it is, it's always slightly dangerous territory when artists address an issue. but. we're not the first, you know. i go, well, what are Shakespeare's plays about? they're about contemporary issues. that's what he wrote about. that's why he was so phenomenal. you can go all the way through the history of art and say well, wait a minute every single artist is in some form or another, is questioning something in their society. and i do think that artists tend to gravitate towards the most important issues of their days, and that's what feeds them. i mean, it's great that journalists are on board, but art, art is open ended. it's never, you know, you never get to the bottom of a good piece of art. it's just, you're forever – it's forever a mystery, which is its charm and, er, its power. and to say, well i've got the answer, is ridiculous. all you have is a part of an answer. if you then wrap into it human activity, you know, you're in a very complicated territory. we're offering human answers. you know, why do you fall in love? it's like yeah, alright, give me an answer to that one   that's why you have a broach church of artists in that sense. you know, Jarvis Cocker makes a pop song, he's going to reach a whole different load of people.

are we going to reach people who vote for Trump? no, we're, probably that's quite difficult. but on the other hand, probably, that's down to us, we should find a way of creating a language that they might get into, i don't know. we're not preaching to the converted, it's up to us to find ways through. i mean it would be nice to make a soap opera. a planet soap opera. Eastenders, for um   that would be great! yeah, i mean, i don't know how many climate stories there are in Eastenders. it takes everything and it's up to us to find the ways of telling stories. that is what we do. and getting them out there. and changing everything. but we, you know, you can't preach. we have this kind of unwritten rule, if we sound like we're preaching, then we stop. i don't sound like i'm preaching do i?

Bertolt Brecht said, 'art has to have wind in its sails.' and you have the wind of the time in your sails. and Bowie would have been inspired by and interested in what's going on. because of course he's a voracious reader, listener to music. and, and movies. all of it. culture. absolutely loves it. so i think he would have been inspired by the music of the time and not felt above it. you know, and it would have crept into what he wanted to do. one of the things he said was 'originality is overrated' which is a really liberating thing. and i think absolutely right. and actually Grayson Perry was saying it recently, like, just stop trying to be original. it's just dumb. it's too late! it's all out there.   just stop it. just try and be good   i bought that a week after he died so that i could play the vinyl. but it's not actually very good. the speakers aren't very good so they, they're not strong enough to pick up the first couple of notes which is really annoying. i just haven't got round to
[*crackles. record starts to play*]

Music: Day after day/They send my friends away/To mansions cold and grey/ To the far side of town/Where the thin men stalk the streets/While the sane stay underground/Day after day/They tell me I can go/They tell me I can blow/To the far side of town/Where it's pointless to be high/'Cause it's such a long way down/ Zane, zane, zane (ah ah ah)/Ouvre le chien/Zane, zane, zane (ah ah ah)/Ouvre le chien

OUVRE LE CHIEN! ha-ha. ah, ah, ah where can the horizon lie   when a nation hides its organic minds! [*low voice*] in a cellar, dark and grim. isn't it good? there's these little touches, like when she goes [*small voice*] 'he followed me home, can i keep him?' and i   remember, just oh! and it's just that – thinking of it now, it's dramatic writing, it's a little bolt of story, it's a ZZ. it's a little girl, and this little kitten or a doggy. and it's things are happening, real people's lives. and listening to his music and because these lyrics are about the world and about people. as opposed to, you know, i like dancing to disco. that's very different. to listening to, you know, a poet in song. and, *lyricist*. if that's the word for a poet who writes songs – a *lyricist* can – not like a novelist, where it has to   there's rules about it. you can explode the rules in a song like you can in a poem. and then touch on things in life. and that little girl [*small voice*] 'he followed me home, can i keep him' oh! I KNOW HER. and i was her, and i've seen her. it's just like, i think about her. ahhh. and just the joy of him dropping that in well just before Christmas 2007, i was sort of unemployed and on income, er, i was on, one of the benefits.   it was just originally a temporary thing. ended up there for eight years. [*laughs*] it was. it was just a job. also, i'd er, i'd been on benefits for quite a while leading up to it and become quite isolated, socially. so it was nice getting out and meeting new people, and a lot of the time it was people i would never have met in the kind of, in the normal social circles. i mean

quite early on i was there i was working with a woman, married an English guy but she came from the Solomon Islands. i'd sit and listen to her tales of canoeing around the Solomon Islands. it was, you know, quite interesting. i did, you know, i quite liked it. it was a pleasant, friendly bunch. having said that, the work was tedious. i knew i was like, probably could do something better with my life, but. but it was, er, keeping me off the dole   and sort of like, it was actually sort of like, nice, a quite nice period of my life, really. i was part-time, and i sort of, i just sort of, because i had, i had kind of really good life balance –i was penniless. [*laughs*] i was on minimum wage, part-time. and er, i was getting housing benefit, what have you. but, it was sort of, i had just started an allotment and stuff like that. and i was tending to my plants during the day and then, going out and hanging around with some nice people at BHS for the rest of the afternoon. it was actually. i was weirdly, quite satisfied with life the player's back stories. you have the Vardy story, which is a rags to riches story. you know, he'd had to play, played in part-time football semi-pro, loading up in a steel works. physical job. then he had to go out and train in the evenings. briefly got arrested for assault when he was, supposedly defending a friend of his in a pub. he had to wear a tag. got put on a curfew. and sometimes had to leave – had to come off the pitch, in a football match, half-way through, so he could rush home, not to break curfew. so then they bring on the sub! i mean, there were several stories, Mark Albrighton was one of them   a very talented player, great professional. he'd also had the summer tragedy. during the summer he'd had the tragedy of losing his mother-in-law, in the Tunisia shooting. so he'd had to recover, come back, and recover after that.   football became a distraction for him. and a way for him to keep his, to distract his family as well. they could see his success, his wife, who lost her mother, could see him succeeding. Mahrez, you know, was bought for four hundred thousand pounds. and people call him 'The Algerian', but he's not. he's a French citizen. he plays for Algeria because his father was Algerian. he was born and bred in Northern Paris. and his father died when he was fifteen. he learnt his football on the streets. he used to climb over the fences to get into football grounds, onto five-a-side pitches to practise his skills. so he wasn't coached. he wasn't picked up at aged eight by some sort of academy, like in Barcelona, you know. a real hunger for it. and then he was told he would never make it into English football because it was too physical, and he was too slight, and so on and so forth. and so he went from club to club. and then you have N'golo Kante, who again comes from a huge family on the outskirts of Paris. a very poor background. plucked out of relative obscurity. and then they came together as a group weirdly, people normally become more right-wing as they get older. i think i've become more left-wing as i've got older. i've always traditionally been, anti-immigration. i don't know if it's from a psychological legacy of fear of the unknown, or being crowded out, or there's not going to be enough room in the world for me, you know. maybe. look i grew up in Leicester.

few Afro-Caribbeans. large Asian population,   Hindu, Sikh and Muslim. and British, white British. it's never been *multi*-cultural, until about, apart from say, last ten years, because of the expansion of the EU. accession to the EU.   Poland and Romania, well, latterly when Romania, but Eastern Bloc expanded, came admitted to the European Union. it's *now* become truly multicultural. i mean, i don't see many South Americans. but it is   and it's, i actually quite like it. i do like it   it's strange, isn't it. i think EU immigration is a good thing, i recognise it as a good thing. i absolutely do, as long it's – i don't want to sound like Tony Blair, but as long as it is positive immigration and it's controlled. because Britain is a small island. i worry about, you know i'm a bit of a NIMBY. i worry about too much house-building, although we're really in need of some of it. covering over the green and pleasant land – i don't like that idea. and i don't think it is all to do with second-home owners, more people, more houses are needed – simple maths. i actually do like, i do like other cultures. do you know what i mean? and i, and i think as long as people integrate. i had an argument one day, a Sikh guy who played in my chess club, a seventy year old, about integration. i think, as long as people integrate i think immigration is great. but my problem is when they don't integrate. in Leicester, in London, in Bradford, wherever it is. in Birmingham, in Manchester, there are huge pockets, where the Muslim community, they just don't integrate. they'll never speak to a white person or a Hindu or a Sikh. you just think – that isn't, that's not what immigration is about no, they're not all Syrian. no, not at all. a high percentage of Syrians were coming. but also big percentage of Afghanis and then others like Iraqis, DRC, Eritrea, Ethiopia even a few. but the main three were Syrians, Afghanis and Iraqis. there was a very clear distinction. the Afghanis,   mostly young men. the Syrians mostly families, a lot of young people but also a big number of families came. mostly those who were waiting for ages for Family Reunion, and then the European didn't give them. so they had no choice except to stay under the bombardment of criminal Assad or, take a boat. so you can see lots of families, lots of babies, lots of children from Syria. and it's like, the conditions. i saw last month, i saw babies, little tiny babies like two months old, sleeping on the mud. and also they were so not used, especially not women, not used to someone like me go on my knee and change her socks. like, make her feel. oh it is different from what you do. you wash your husband's feet in Syria. and then i heard once a woman, in her sixties or something, saying, 'a man! a man changed my shoes! imagine how humane they are!' and stuff. also the baby. i changed a baby once. a family came all wet, the baby like two months. i grabbed the baby. put him on a mat and changed the nappy. and the woman was going, 'no! you are a man! you are a man! you can't do that!' and i said to her, 'i do that. i've been doing that for years'. i remember one day – we had in one place ninety-six boats, average between fifty to sixty people. in one place. it's called Molyvos, or Eftalou. and this is the dirt road where people came. and it's one of the most difficult places because not too many cars. so if you land somewhere you have to walk. the only people who give you a hand are volunteers with their cars. no organisations, no UNHCR, no governments, nothing. nothing! no government, except i think in November the Swedish government sent a medical team for one week. and then, and then the Scottish sent a few ambulances. i got out of the water all wet, and i saw, yes, ambulances. NHS Scotland! yay! viva Scotland!

well, *my* pitch is that it's brought peace to Europe. we tried living as a bunch of nation-states in Europe. we failed completely. it's time for something better. we can break down barriers. we can get closer together as peoples. we can be more prosperous   and *their* pitch was that Cameron's renegotiation deal gives us the best of both worlds. we are in the bits of the EU that we like, and we're not in the bits that we don't like.   it didn't sell. because we didn't have enough time to – we'd spent ten years attacking the EU and all its works, so you can't credibly come back and say: it's brilliant, we need to stay in this! so we were left saying: well, we've got some reforms.   'it's bureaucratic, it's corrupt, it's a superstate, it's oppressing us', and then you suddenly flip around and say, well, it's necessary. we basically made the argument for colonial occupation that colonial authorities always made: we know you don't like the overlordship, but   overlordship is more efficient essentially that was our slogan. keep up the East India Company! the Tory party in the 1890s had a slogan in Ireland called 'killing Home Rule with kindness.'   we weren't even trying to kill Home Rule with kindness, here. we were trying to kill it with threats of World War 3. 'Project Fear' was the only argument we had, and 'Project Fear' could've worked, probably, if we'd made it scary. but we wanted to say it would be really, really scary, while at the same time   saying that it was entirely reasonable for the Education Secretary

to be a complete lunatic who was bringing the country into destruction while not firing the Education Secretary. and because we didn't – you know, we couldn't go for a full-throated attack on members of the Cabinet – meant we couldn't use 'Project Fear' as it should've been used i wanted to tell you about the night boats. mostly the night boats were taken by Afghanis because they are poor. poorer. and it's cheaper. it's cheaper, they are poorer and also every country has their own smugglers. so like, from my research, the most cruel smugglers were the Afghanis. they were very cruel. to their own people. so they came on the night, and also we were able to recognise because they gave them cheap lifejackets. they came with the blue ones which are very cheap, while the Syrians mostly came with orange. if people came straight, it's very close. it's like a six kilometre trip. if the waves, if the sea is calm and the waves are really low: one hour or less. but then. mostly ninety-five percent of drivers, the people who drive the boats, they are refugees. and they were forced to drive boat. so the smuggler picked you up, and you drive it. you can't say no. you can't say no. so they take you for one go around, and they say, like, it's easy. and then you end up, like, sometimes you come here, aim to this one, and you end up here. and it's scary. it's like, i went on the boat twice, three times, and it's very scary. but we, by that time we developed, the volunteers, we developed skills as well. so we saw the boat and we know, we knew exactly where the boat was going. so we could judge the waves. we waited there. and also we created WhatsApp groups, and we'd say a boat is moving to the left to this spot. so we kind of developed the skills. but if you come on a nice day it takes an hour, one and a half hours. if you come at night, in one way it's good because you can see the lights. you know that you are going somewhere. and we started, for example, making some campfires – a big fire. so they follow the fire. it is, with the Afghanis it was more, more difficult. they'd never been on the water ever it's a really good question. and it's one i've sort of wrestled with   because, if we'd have voted to become an Islamic state, and it was like a, but hang on, 'it was a popular vote'. would we have no recourse to change it? you know what i mean? 'now you've got to wear a headscarf' – i'd be like. but we've not voted to become. i don't know. i don't know. i don't really know, i kind of see both sides of the argument. i do. but i don't agree with this notion that we should vote until we get the right result. that's what annoys me. and i know you're not here to listen to me to try and lobby for Leave, you're here to listen to my reasons for Leaving, and they are that, the European Union i think, was originally the coal and steel industry, wasn't it? a coal and steel industry, between France and Germany. to try, you know after the war, the second world war. to try and figure out, alright, let's have it. common ground here in trade. and it has just grown and grown and grown. and the more and more and more you grow a club, the less it becomes elite. and i just think, well, where does it stop? there was talk of Morocco at one stage, becoming part of the European Union, and then Turkey   and then, that borders. Turkey borders Iran, Iraq, Syria, so then, where does it stop? i did not want to go down that rabbit hole. so, i think we needed a sort of watershed moment, where we go, 'enough is enough'   actually if we leave, we've got a once in a lifetime chance to leave, let's take it now, so at least we can have our own sovereignty and be masters of our own destiny i mean the police is not great. they used to be great. last time i visit i saw a policeman hitting somebody for no reason. somebody standing and a policeman jumped on him and hit him with his two legs. i called, what do you call the donkey thing here? the hoof? i called it like, with his two hooves, like, for no reason because he was upset with somebody. but locals, the big majority are very nice, very, very nice. there is a little part of the community that are like fascists. they have some party called Golden Dawn. but then if these guys attack the refugees, the Greek attack the Golden Dawn people. people are very good to them. i believe better than any other European country. the EU can do much, much better. i mean they have sixty-thousand people stuck for years. they can speed up, for example, the Family Reunion, which is families waiting to be reunited. for example, their partner's in Europe, why don't you just take them? they will go eventually. Germany took a million. but i don't think sixty-thousand is a big difficult number. what are they doing now? they force people to deal with smugglers. i mean the councils in Germany gave them houses depending on the family members in Greece. so if you have a wife in Greece and three children, they gave you four bedroom. and you live alone with all this bedroom, waiting for your family. so, why does Germany make it so difficult for them to get there?

you know what it felt like? it felt like if you were watching a romantic comedy and, the wedding to the wrong person just happens. [*laughs*] it isn't supposed to happen. and so, i just feel like, i was just so, staring at it and this is such a shitshow and i can't even articulate why it's a shitshow. it's interesting to see all of these people protesting and trying to change things. but it's also disheartening to see the things that we're arguing about. like, i feel like we are wasting so much energy. to me there's nothing more depressing than these incredible teenagers having to orchestrate a huge march so that we put basic regulations on guns? it's nuts. and then just that the fact that the first thing that he launched into was the Muslims ban. i was like, oh great. really? and i think actually that was also a running refrain throughout the campaign. it was like, 'oh, he's just saying that, he's not really going to do that'. but it's like *well*, you know he's saying the thing because it's working. like, Trump in a lot of ways, i doubt he personally understands the internet. but he's got people around him who understand the internet. i guess Steve Bannon figured this out with Breitbart. when you're, when you're working online, your way of creating content is to throw spaghetti at the wall and see what sticks. and that's what he did with his approach to trying to win, he just threw a bunch of ideas, like, racist ideas. it was like a racist salad. and some of it stuck. and it's like, people really hate Muslims right now. and i don't know how to deal with that

he's just not an artful communicator. i
don't think he has a racist bone in his
body. but i think one would have to look
at what's going on in the world. in the
Middle East.   the fears that are going
on in neighbouring countries. where
women in Finland are being advised
to stay in after nine o'clock. for fear of
horrific things happening. certainly, the
Middle East hasn't cornered the market on
this. there's people everywhere. but in
terms of your question, how he, all he
wants is a reasoned policy towards
immigration. anybody that wants to come
in and can bring value to this country, let's
do it. but you have to check in at the door.
so i don't think he's a racist. i think he's
pragmatic. but, the media is going to,
anything he does they're going to attack.
they just hate him with the fire of a
thousand suns. he's not going to get a fair
shake. but i don't think he's racist. i
wouldn't have voted for him if i thought
he was racist. racism is evil. you cannot be
a Christ follower and believe in racism.
and you can't hate people who are same-
sex attracted. you can't hate them if you're
a Christian. now, you can have, um, you
can have a biblical stance upon the actions,
but the actions and the person are
completely and totally different. that's a
soul. that's someone you have to love

it's like being, saying you're a bloody paedophile or something. i mean – really! really, it's a stigma   i have sort of, what i call, imaginary friends on Facebook. and i was constantly, i was like a one man, it was me versus about fifty people at times   and what they did, the tactics they used, was sort of like, someone would ask me questions and wait for me to trip up. because it's such a complicated issue, isn't it? referendums. you don't, i don't have all the answers. on, you know, the future, on economics, on society,

on whatever it might be. nobody does. but rather than me asking them questions, i fell into the trap of just spouting my mouth off. sometimes in an eloquent way, but sometimes in a sort of like, fuck you way. it became quite er   as i say, toxic.

a lot of people de-friended me   i would be talking about immigration, for example, and people would say, well, you need a vibrant, young population to support the economy and this that and the other. and i'd be like, i'd be talking about redundant immigration and house-building and infrastructure. and you know, all the rest of it. and, really really bad. it got really nasty. really pernicious. and the inevitable magic word came out of racist. and for a start, i'm like, it's xenophobia – but i'm not xenophobic. but i am, i am, i don't like the idea of overpopulation, i never have. even right from a young age. even from the age of about twelve, i've been like, quite fixated by over-population. yeah people were angry. leave voters were very angry. just, angry. i mean, it wasn't. they had been – i suppose given permission to voice all of their frustrations at the Remain campaign. about immigration, economic insecurity, the cultural rule of the cities   and they felt that voting Leave would release them all. Camberley is the one that really sticks in my mind for this   a fifty year old woman nearly clocking the guy i was canvassing with, for no apparent reason. just for being on the wrong side. it was   it was a real visceral sense of people's difficult lives – bursting at this point. and the Leave campaign – and this is something that Remainers didn't really understand and haven't understood since – was a campaign of hope and emancipation. it's come into memory as 'take back control,' but they didn't say 'take back control,' they said, 'take control.' so, go out into the world, vote Leave, take control   it was   this thing is holding us back. we're shackled to a corpse, as they sometimes said. which is actually language that goes back to 1948 and the original attempts at European unification and Britain saying, well we shouldn't be shackled to this corpse. and at the time that referred to the war-destroyed Europe. and now it was being repurposed for the Eurozone crisis we were just in a daze like, how the hell did this just happen?   crazy because you walked around New York and you felt – everyone's sad. everyone, it felt like everyone had the wind knocked out of them. my dad said that every person that rode in his Uber felt, like, ashamed. one of my cousins who wears hijab, she was like, you know, during the election it was fine, generally. obviously there are a lot of Trump supporters in North Carolina, but, you know, she, she said that then, after he won, it felt like then things got more racist. because the racists were all, 'yeah, we're in power now'. and i feel like for me, it felt like such a fuck you to see – i think that my city didn't come out for Trump but, my state did. and i felt like, like my state had betrayed me. am i not from you? or it was like a confirmation that i wasn't from there. i think Trump became a mirror for this country of all the things – because you had all these people that were giving this like, 'this is not who we are' thing. and i was like *well*, this is who you've always been, and you just, kind of, don't wanna deal with it. and now you have to deal with it. and i feel like, Hilary, in a lot of ways, if she'd won, you know, this was going to happen sooner rather than later well. she, she just hates everything that i believe in. and believes in everything that i – don't   i believe, i believe in the sanctity of life, but – not just for the unborn. but that people deserve to live with dignity until they take their last breath. and, she does not. she believes in a much more   socialistic form of government which.   i think, has been proven to be, fairly acceptable in smaller countries, but in a country as gigantic as ours – i just don't trust my government that much.

and, um, gosh, she's just, such an unpleasant person. i can't wait to turn,   to vote for a female. but she is not that one, she is not the one. so, it was strictly one hundred percent on her values. and, i'm not really a conspiracy theorist but, gosh, there is certainly a lot of smoke around the Clintons, in terms of, people shooting themselves in the head twice. which seems remarkable. a lot of people wind up not alive around them. so, if, if. i guess that that would be it. i just find her, i wish her well, but i'm glad she's not our leader. she is smart. she could run a country. there are a lot of things she could do. um, but, i can assure you. you know it's funny how people have such short memories. she was disgusted by Trump – her husband was just a scoundrel in his behaviour, when it comes to, i mean just *horrible*. far, far worse than anything Trump did   maybe Hilary is, i mean you know, she loves, she raised Chelsea. Chelsea – even though i disagree with her politics, she's a nice young person. so, who knows, if i met Hilary under completely different circumstances i might think she's the most charming person in the world

Liane Carroll jazz music playing in the background throughout] Carrie Fisher! take one! wishful drinking! she died when she was sixty, didn't she? she was only a few years older than me. her first husband was the lovely Paul Simon, who she went out with for many years, and then they got married. the marriage broke up within a year because she said Paul Simon said she made a better girlfriend than a wife. and she quoted this song that Paul Simon wrote about it   it's called 'Allergies.' she quoted the lyric that goes something like *i'm allergic to the woman i love*   um   *i'm allergic to the woman i love.* i can't remember the next line. she said, you know, hearing something like that was just devastating. and she said i married a short Jewish guy, so basically i married my father. a short Jewish guy who sings, and that's what i did. i married my father. and she hadn't talked to her father for years and years and years. then she got back together with him just before her father died, and she was very grateful for that. but i didn't realise that Gary, the dog, Gary Fisher who was her constant companion, was actually an emotional support dog. he wasn't just a dog that she collected from the pound. he was trained as an emotional support dog, which is, it's quite something. it's like seeing somebody walking around with a crutch for a broken leg, but they're walking around with a pet for a mental health debility. but   this thing about not understanding what anybody sees in you is really strong in her life i just think that she should have fully embraced the fact that he was totally wrong. i think that she should have been actually left. i think she should have been an actual leftist. i think she tried too hard, she did the same thing that, that er, what's his face, er. oh god, Miliband, sorry. i almost called him sandwich man. [*laughs*] but she did the same thing that he did wrong i think, to pander too much to the centre. like, if she had let Bernie be more of her indicator than Trump, then i think she probably would have won. because i do think that, like, there, there's been a lot of people crying out for a genuine left here. but she's also genuinely a centrist, i think. and i think that another thing

like, i don't think it's wrong to say that gender mattered in that situation too. because i do think that, like, this country is also insanely sexist and backwards. you know, this country. i don't know, i don't think we can handle having a female president yet. i mean i think it was one factor in a bunch of craziness. but if you had for example, Joe Biden as the candidate – i think that he would have beaten Trump. not because he was a better candidate than Hilary, but because people would have seen it as grandpa calming down the crazy guy. but you know, i mean, that's also something that i didn't want to accept either. because it's like, oh. i mean, i don't want, i never want to vote for a woman just because it's a woman. but i do think that the fact she was a woman had its role to play

she'd done Shampoo where she played a
sexually precocious girl who came onto Warren Beatty.
she was already drinking and i think she was probably on
diet pills. and she had this image of her face as being
incredibly wide. and when she did Leia they put great big
buns on it and made it even wider. she was the only
woman on Star Wars, really, on the cast. she said it's
interesting that George Lucas created this space world
with no women in it. she said she was the only one. and
there was one night in a bar where they were all getting
lairy and she was being made very well aware that she was
the plaything. she was going to be passed around them all.
which was when apparently Harrison stepped in and said,
'hey, the little lady doesn't like what's happening,' and
took her outside. and then pounced on her. that's
when their affair began. this dysfunctional affair with this
man who was cold and unresponsive. but of course she
responded to that because that's what she was used to
with her father and her home life is that you fall in love
with a man who doesn't give anything back to you. she
writes about it in such a way that it's all her fault for not
being funny enough and not being cute enough. if only
she'd said something better to him, then he would've.

you can hear it's an incredibly familiar tale. it's
accommodating a man's feelings. if only i could make him
feel more comfortable then he'd open up to me. if only i
could be funny enough, then he'd feel more relaxed and
then he'd love me more. it's extraordinary

oh boy, do i. he, i think has been misquoted
and misunderstood on this. and the reason i
think that is because. i, i just think, you know,
it's cliché but sometimes clichés continue to
exist because there is truth in them. actions do
speak louder than words and if you look at
how he ran his companies – it was one
hundred percent on who's going to make him
the most money! i mean, you cannot. you
cannot – trust me on this, i was in this industry
for years – you cannot really work in the hotel
or restaurant industry and be either racist or a
homophobe. you cannot. it just lends itself
you know, it didn't matter. are you good? do
you do a good job? do you present yourself
well? are you personable? great   part of it
also is, a lot of those things that he's been
accused of, he's actually been vindicated. now
certainly he said those contemptible and
ridiculous and sophomoric and sixth grade
things, um, in an unguarded moment on that
bus. but the thing that people sort of missed
in that, even though it was horrific, was that
he did say 'and they let me'. so with that
assumption of an implied consent, if we are to
believe part of the horrible or, all of the
horrible things, you also have to believe that
as well. and as one who has served the
unbelievably rich in a former business. i have
seen lots of women who have, just been. it's
just crazy what they will allow to be done with
them. just to be near either celebrity or wealth.
so. so, so, i dunno

you know, it's funny you say that, because, on the one hand, i've just said this to you. that you know, it's the first time i've actually articulated it that way, to be honest. . . because one thing that drives me nuts about this whole Brexit thing is so many, say, MPs, know it's going to be a disaster. *know*, a lot of businesses *know*

and people are not speaking up. and people are afraid to speak up. now, whether they're afraid to speak up because, er, they just don't want to get a drubbing by The Daily Mail. or, whether it's more sinister. i wouldn't, i wouldn't want to say. but i do think we're in a really weird place in the UK. i think that people are, not comfortable just saying it as it is. and we've almost indulged in this, like, political speak of people, kind of, going around issues and not, not being in a straight line towards what they're actually meaning to say. on the one hand, normal people in the country like it when people are direct and clear, and not faffing around like a politician. on the other hand, when people are direct and clear, they risk at least verbal abuse and press abuse, and possibly more gratuitous stuff   look at a lot of the abuse female in particular MPs. they've had death threats. they've had a lot of attacks. i actually think we've got a massive problem of misogyny in this country   we think we're sort of, progressive. modern? and i actually think we're very, very far behind. very far behind on, not only gender, on all sorts of diversity fronts i can't remember what order it came in. but they kept saying there was going to be like a white knight saviour. someone was going to swoop in and buy it all up. there was a lot of talk of Mike Ashley, Sports Direct, taking over at one point. that's when i, that's when i did start straight away looking for alternative employment. people had started looking for work at other places. there was a Wilco that had opportunistically opened just, well they had the open day kind of two days after BHS shut or something.

i went for an interview there. yeah, but er, it didn't go well. i was, i didn't have what it took to be a Wilco employee. i was told i didn't, er, what was it. there was a question, you know like the sort of interview questions you get, 'tell us a time when you've gone above and beyond the call of duty to offer excellent customer service'   i just sort of looked at him and shrugged my shoulders. [*laughs*] i didn't get the job   'oh yeah. i did a beautiful job. i made those towels look so neat. i'm fairly positive it encouraged at least one person to buy a flannel when she wasn't originally going to'. i mean this is the weird thing working in retail. the kind of like, just this, the level of bullshit. you know when you're just, you're opening boxes and putting stuff out on shelves, but there's this whole sort of, David Brent-ish kind of jargon attached to everything now. how much you're supposed to care about it all *laughs*] it's one of those words that you read a lot that journalists use but i don't think anyone uses it in real life. i don't know, maybe hard-core fans do call themselves the Corbynistas, but i've never been, if that's the case, then i've never been a hardcore fan   i've never heard anyone say Corbynista in real life. i'd forgotten about it until you just said it   yeah. it's a little bit like, i can see maybe they brainstormed to come up with it at Labour HQ. and they're like, 'let's give him a name, like, the beehive for Beyonce.   Corbyn's Corbynistas' it's hard, gosh. i never blame anybody for how, for having a distorted view of how it is here. because we, we provide that for them. through the media. i would think America was a crazy, insane, murder-filled, jingoistic country too   you know Ronald Reagan once said, looking at yourself in the media, is kind of like seeing yourself in a fun house

i met a guy in distribution, and one of his clients was one of Trump's hotels. and so he asked the person with who he normally dealt with, he said, what's he really like? she said, 'i am a butch' – these are her words, not mine, 'i am a butch lesbian, and he treats me wonderfully when he comes in. and he makes sure that people like me are part of his organisation. because he doesn't care. he's looking for brilliance and hard work.' he doesn't care. black. white. short. fat. old. young. gay. straight. doesn't care. can you make him money? and, that's kind of the American way. that's true conservatism. saying, let's get out of identity politics. let's focus on what you can do and are you doing it well?

and i think i kind of got all worked
up as well because i could see, what
the newspapers were doing against
him   and all the newspapers
started, like i think, it was then they
were saying things about him. or was
it David Cameron said, 'get a tie'. you
know, things like that. all kind of
added to this image that i had of him,
as, he's finally someone who isn't like
mainstream politicians. i felt you
could trust him completely. and even
when he made mistakes, and people
said he's not very charismatic or
whatever, and i was like, but at least
he seems kind of truthful. and he
seemed quite kind. i'm trying to
remember actual headlines, because
it was, it's all getting mixed up now
with when it was the big election.
because then the newspapers were
even worse. but. i can't remember if
Tony Blair at that point had said
something negative. but he popped
up out of nowhere saying it'd be
really bad. erm, Alan Sugar, i
remember saying, it'd be awful for
the Labour Party. and it just, was all
the kind of same-aged men, who
are doing really well for themselves,
saying, it'll be a disaster

i feel like it's because they think that the 'fake news media' is – well he's convinced them that they are at war. and so they think that everything is not true. it's crazy that such a, developed country, is filled with, you know, i want to say stupid people, but it's – so many people that have become manipulated. it's such a privilege to live in a country where everyone is. i mean obviously there's still problems with all sorts of things, but at least it's relatively transparent and democratic, and we have all these institutions. but then, especially coming from, you know my, my family – the way that people sound now they sound like they're in the Middle East. and people in the Middle East have a legitimate reason to believe conspiracy theories, right? and like, you know, things happen. like, for Palestinians – Israelis do really weird shit to Palestinians. all sorts of like, weird, putting things in the water. and, you know, my cous – my uncle, the settlers set wild boars onto their land. so he *says* that, but then my – i've heard that this isn't necessarily true. that wild boars have like, arisen. i dunno. but if you exist in a society where you have no neutral source of information you, you create conspiracy theories. but in a country where we have very good journalism, we don't *need* conspiracy theories. but: Infowars has an insane amount of traffic i was obsessed with the BBC being impartial. but actually, even Richard Littlejohn and commentators like that have said, the BBC did a remarkable job of remaining neutral. but i, i was like on paranoid overdrive. they did a thing for Remain which was great. i thought, you manipulative bastards. and then they did a thing for Leave, it was on Michael Gove, and it was about fishing, something to do with fishing or whatever. i was thinking, who gives a fuck about fishing. it's irrelevant, it doesn't affect anybody. you're just dumbing down and, or focusing on irrelevancy. that's not going to sway anybody, or reflect Leavers concerns. you know, and i, i became quite paranoid over it. do you know what i mean? i was obsessed with the BBC   i don't know what newspapers, i simply don't know. what media? maybe ITV, because some of the debates were quite good and it reflected, you know, it was a bit identity politics, but it reflected the arguments quite well. i took most notice of the broadcast representation. whereas, print journalism, press barons or whatever. or of social media, because that's just like the wild west isn't it?   i de-sensitised, i just think, hurry up. i do get annoyed when i hear for example, that the House of Lords have quashed a bill, or whatever it is, i just think, you unelected gits. what are you doing? and it does annoy me, when the likes of. i think we're paying far too much deference to bloody celebrities. you know even the BBC now, are saying 'oh politicians and celebrities are calling for' – what? celebrities are 'calling for' – are they? are they really? well so what. sing or act. great. but i don't, don't give them any authority – i blame John Lennon. i've got a John Lennon tattoo. it all started with him, honestly the night after the election, was it 2017? when they got loads more votes than people thought, my office is actually near Labour headquarters. so me and this girl went and stood outside, cos we knew he was going to come out, because he had been up there all night. so we were cheering for him. and then i'd woken up really excited and i'd put like a red top on, and red lipstick. and me and my friends was all excited. and the BBC was there. they're like, can we speak to you? and we were like, yeah, so they were interviewing us about Jeremy Corbyn. and then it was on the six o'clock news. and my friends were texting me. and i remember she was saying, why are you excited? and i was talking. and then she went, 'but Labour haven't won.' and i was like, yeah. and i was like, oh no, do i sound like i thought Labour won? but i was so pleasantly surprised that they'd got more seats

i didn't stay up to watch it. and i deleted my Facebook actually as well, because i was like, i can't bear all the bad news. and then when i woke up in the morning. it was like a lovely surprise! and i was really excited and went and we were cheering him, and there was loads of people. well not loads of people, there was like twenty people cheering him. but there was loads of cameras all surrounding him. so that was nice i mean, getting coverage, but also getting more excitement. people made it seem like Trump was the product of being covered by outlets. and i feel like, there's always room to scrutinise how he was covered. but i also think that people don't want to acknowledge the fact that   he represented a lot of things that have been brewing in the US for a really long time. that people just didn't want to acknowledge what was happening here. people do have a lot of, like, fear of immigrants and fear of different people. you know, all these different kinds of anxieties. and he totally ripped the curtain away from that. and i mean, i feel like i, not accepted but, i realised that he was probably going to win when i stopped being in denial about it. i was like, oh yeah, this is happening.   i would read like, a hot take, to make myself feel better. but the week before i felt that it was, i just thought he was going to win. and i remember i was like, i was talking to some people at work and they were like, yeah Hilary's going to win, and it was like, i don't know. and i think it was because i was running the twitter account for work. and like, i don't think that's a coincidence. and obviously part of it was probably, you know, now that we know more about the whole Russia-meddling thing, that maybe a lot of them were bots. um, but, it just felt like there was just so much more excitement for Trump   i think the thing is that we separate the online world from the real world, when actually i think that they're the same thing, and that the things we see on the internet, you know, we should take it seriously. and i, you know, i feel like it matters a lot more than we think it does. i shouldn't be surprised if the Trump campaign had a better understanding of the part of the internet that is driving the most traffic. Trump seemed to electrify people in a way that Obama did. except it was like, you know, evil

---

it was a terrorist attack. it was a politically
motivated attack. which is shocking in and of
itself. and   that's the actions of a person, but i
do think you can get contexts that fan the flames.
and i do think that we have seen, we have seen a
lot more of that in previous years. and i think we
have seen a sort of level of desperation in our
political discourse, around immigration, Brexit,
that certainly doesn't help that context. and i
think that's another reason why people
potentially, people are attracted to that phrase
                                    'we've got more in
common than that which divides us' because, it
seems to be like an anti-politics statement. it's an
anti-debate, and it's, let's not disagree, let's find
the common ground. which is important, but it's
also important to find, i think, a way of having
the debates that is more respectful and, er, allows
people to air their points of view without,
frankly, creating a culture and an environment in
which it becomes hostile. what, in so far as, Jo's
murder has influenced me, as someone who
deeply loved her, deeply admired her   she, she
was brave. she was very brave. and she did things
that i thought about, and thought, oh, i don't
think i'm brave enough. but i think her, murder,
sort of compelled me to – to feel like well, i need
    i want to speak out about what i find important
    to slightly stick my neck out. i don't, i don't
want her murder to silence people. because
there's a danger of people thinking that, like it's
too scary for women in particular to speak out
on anything. and it shouldn't be that way. and we
need to, if we give in to that then we'll be run by
a patriarchal society of quite posh old men that
don't really relate to most of the country. for
decades to come

45

i dunno. it's tough. man, we
are, you know as a nation, our
politics has involved *duels*.
people go, oh we've never
been more separate in our
lives, i'm like – read the history
books! this is the norm in
America. we have always had
very spirited debate   i
thought this country was done.
you know, Margaret Thatcher
had a pretty great saying, she
said that democracy only
works until people realise that
they can vote themselves to
the top. she said it another
way, but that was the point. we
as a nation, are getting pretty
close to the point where there
are more people in the wagon
than pulling the wagon. and
those people in the wagon
get to vote, so i. i, i just didn't
think we had one more in us,
you know. remember, all this is
from my perspective

like that's, you know the thing that's hard for democrats to accept, or that other Americans to accept, is that there are a lot of people in this country that have been left behind. obviously not all those people voted for Trump, and i feel like that narrative is a little too clean. i feel like people voted all sorts of different ways, and there's probably a lot of people who didn't even vote. i don't know how this election would have turned out like, if, if we had higher voter turnout. because a lot of people just don't see anything change. they vote for Obama, they vote for Trump, they vote for Bush, they vote for Clinton — they vote for whoever, and their life stays exactly the same there obviously was a kick the bastards element of it. but there was also a thing saying no, we're Britain, we can go out there, we can do amazing stuff. we're a great historical country, and we can – it would tinge into arrogance sometimes

say well, we're so good everyone's going to have to bow down to us and treat us better. but there was a real sense that outside the EU Britain would be capable of a whole lot more than it was capable of inside the EU. we saw from our polling that about half of Leave voters didn't think anything bad would happen from leaving. so, they weren't judging positive and negative outcomes. they just thought it's all going to be brilliant i did. my fixed idea was vote Leave   when he announced the Referendum, my immediate reaction was, 'yeah, course! vote fucking Leave, of course!' because i'm, i'm, i like to bloody the nose. i'm a bit of a reactionary   i do like to, a bit of a protest, you know. i'm 'burn the Reichstag!' i am a little bit like that. and i don't think these things through properly. that reflects in my chess. and yeah, yeah, let's vote Leave. and, the more and more i considered it, up to the Referendum day, i thought, you know what – my heart does say Leave, but i can actually think of more reasons to vote to stay. to remain. so on the day, i was like, 'i'm not sure, i haven't decided.'   i was nailed on Leave, right up. and then on the day, i was like   the thing that swayed me, is the arrogant buggers on Facebook. the Remainers, the Islington elite. you know, that were sort of looking down their nose at people   it became personal rather than political. and this idea that the older generation shouldn't have a vote because it's not their future. well, hang on, how can you say that to a sixty-five year old? they're still going to be alive for another twenty-five years. what, are they just going to die, are they? do they not count? no. bollocks. and also, they've paid into the economy for all that time, so surely they should. we're all equal in that sense. but, i, when Cameron – this is a very important point as far as i'm concerned, said that the government would be spending nine million pounds, or was it eight million? nine million pounds, on a Remain campaign. i hit the roof. because that's – if you live in a democracy, a referendum should be neutral. the government should have a neutral position, rather than a subjective. and he said, well the government takes a position on it so why wouldn't we spend money. but that's taxpayers money. so that sealed the deal for me. up until voting day when i thought, you know what, i haven't thought this through properly, because   this could be a right mess. and i didn't know, just how messy it would be. i'm sick of hearing about it, you know what i mean? the weird thing is, that a lot of people who voted Leave woke up the next morning, thinking that it was going to go back to 1961. you know, pre-Beatles, kind of like, everybody's white. sorry, that, you know – the horse has bolted. that is never going to happen do i still feel like the Conservatives should be in government?' are they in government? 'is there a government?' is a question that's worth asking i am a, lifetime, er, conservative, whatever that means, constitutionalist perhaps? um, who, has been a reliable conservative voter since i was eighteen. so, for thirty years. and um so, yes. this election while it brought [*laughs*] its own challenges, was, probably not as difficult, not as difficult a decision for me as perhaps it was for some. consistently Republican. but that's because, they presented a better candidate in my view. here in Albuquerque we had a mayor who was a Democrat and he served, a lifetime, and he was absolutely fantastic, and i would definitely have voted for him. he was a, really good, he just ran the city well. so, i, i would vote for a Democrat, should the best Democrat come along   um, but i er, i sort of see things because of my faith. um, which is no secret. i sort of view things through the lens of scripture. and, so, whichever candidate aligns themselves most, most closely – in terms of *policy*, not in terms of personal behaviour. and it's tough to separate those two sometimes. but just in terms of what they say they will do, or what they can be relied upon to do, is how i make my decisions so, so i've always been Labour. and like, my family's always been Labour   but i didn't actually know that much about politics before 2016. i was more, like, from an ideology point of view. i was always, i'm left-wing, i'm Labour. like, me and my friends say there is nothing worse than a northern Tory, and i think being northern is part of it as well but i didn't know that much about individual politicians. erm, i wasn't reading that much about politics. which now, i don't know how i escaped it, because now it's kind of on every website i read

so then when i heard about Jeremy Corbyn, i had to get my friends to tell me about him because i'd never heard of him ever. i'm trying to remember now   one of my most political friends. she kind of, erm, was sending me, like, headlines and things, WhatsApp groups   so i guess i just, it was my friends talking about him. and then i started to notice things in newspapers.   then, i would start arguing with people. i remember my mum asking me oh, but do you think he could lead the Labour Party though? do you think he could do that? like, yeah. and i was like, because the things that, the qualities that people think you need to be a leader in politics, hasn't gone very well, hasn't got us very far. and i thought at the time, he's so left-wing, and the Tories have gone so right wing, that i was like, surely, it's good to have the yin and the yang?

i had been a Pearson fan. i liked Pearson. objections to Pearson were largely because of his public persona, which he hadn't got right. rude to the press. he was quite uncommunicative, could appear quite surly in interviews. but i thought that, any – and a lot of people thought that he was complacent when Leicester were bottom of the league and looked like going to get relegated, and he kept saying, oh, we can still turn this around. and i thought that he was self-deceiving really, but he turned out to be absolutely right. and he did turn it around. and i thought any manager that can do that, why get, you know, what on earth? why sack a manager who has just finished the season with a run like that? it was a weird thing to do. and it may have had more to do with just relationships. also, the kerfuffle around Pearson's son got caught in the scandal in Thailand, because his son had been seeing call girls and filming it i didn't particularly have a choice. i would have preferred, i probably would have gone for an English manager. somebody who spoke good English who could relate to a team which had a strong English core. i thought it was a very odd choice. but he was experienced and played it, just perfect. the way that Ranieri played that season. because he didn't raise hopes. he just said, let's dream, and you know, he was a real gent made a good spirit within the club and within the team. and he was, you know his big thing was, i want clean sheets. he wasn't sort of saying, we can win, score goals, he was letting his attackers get on with it. but he kept on saying, all i want is a clean sheet! it seemed to be more important than the result, almost and he said if it's clean sheets, it's pizzas all round. i'm going to buy them pizzas no, absolutely not. he wasn't even on the list. he, he was not in my top 3. he, i was not ra-ra Trump from the beginning at all   this sort of, cartoonish caricature with the comb over, this You're Fired! i didn't know what he, he was about. i knew that he had run in liberal and Democrat circles in the past, so i didn't know that i could trust him to, vote my, with some, with some degree of reliability for what the Republicans are about. but as i heard him speak, i thought, well, anybody can say anything, but it looks like he might be trustworthy. or at least, i don't know. once he became our candidate, i threw everything behind him, because the alternative was just terrifying. um, here's what i've told people. because, i deal with young Czech people, they are young and idealistic. they want to know about America. so what i tell them, because they always want to know what i think about Trump and what i used to think about Obama. so i tell them, if i lived in a cul-de-sac and Trump and Obama were my neighbours, i would probably like Obama a lot more. Obama would be my favourite neighbour. and Trump would probably be somebody that i would try to get away from. so, so it's not really about personality so much with him. but the things that he, the personality traits that are important to me, anyway, he actually does have. he genuinely, truly loves this country. now he may, he may communicate badly. really badly. and it may look jingoistic to an outsider, because he's just a big, tough, brash New Yorker. but, he, he really likes us. and i didn't get that from Obama

Dominic Chapell, we had no actual reason to believe that he wasn't genuine, because we knew nothing about him. he was like this mad Walter Mitty lunatic character   just a, sort of like, privileged, like con man lunatic, whose dad. well he says his dad worked at er, selling oil to, i dunno. he says he's had dinner with Colonel Gaddaffi, i don't know, he also told everyone he was in the SAS, and he was a racing driver. i see him, he's sort of like the clown of the piece, isn't he. he's like, he just sort of thought he could come in and, and he had some sort of vague understanding of what Phillip Green was doing, that you can have BHS, run it into the ground and fill your pockets, but he didn't even know how to do it properly. he was just sort of like, literally went in there and wrote himself cheques. oh, i think i'll buy myself a helicopter. just write himself a cheque. i don't think he actually bought himself a helicopter. he was that sort of thing though. when he, when he, first one of the court cases he had, he turned up and said, 'i'm sorry, i wasn't aware i'd been summonsed because i was on my yacht'. which is a really bad defence, i think, in the circumstances. just don't, i mean. anything to do with BHS, don't mention a yacht, whoever you are. like i say, you've got Phillip Green, the full-on villain, and Dominic Chappell just a sort of clown character. the little comic relief of the piece.   he's just an incompetent idiot. whereas, whatever you say about Phillip Green, no matter what he does, he's an absolute genius. but as a human being, he's a fucking dismal failure. just on every level

i don't know why that is because it's
not like Jeremy Corbyn is, is a young cool
guy. but i guess it's, like, cos i work in
advertising and the buzzword is
millennials, millennials, millennials and
everyone's like, millennials just want
authenticity, they'll see through
everything. and i wonder if actually there
is something to that. maybe it was the
authentic thing. erm, and he was a bit of
an underdog. and the more that the right-
wing newspapers, it was basically right-
wing newspapers, were tearing him down,
saying it would be a disaster. but i didn't
vote for him to like, it wasn't like a protest
vote. i genuinely thought he would be a
great leader. like i was saying before, when
people were saying the leadership
qualities. and i was like, oh, i never know
any of the leadership experience of any of
the politicians. it's not like i've been
through everyone's CV and have seen
how all these politicians have managed
people. i don't know anything about
them. all you can vote for really is what
they're saying, what they stand for, and
their actions

i feel like Trump, Trump was basically like a little kid standing in front of his whole school for a talent show, and was just getting a reaction from what he was saying and it didn't matter if it was good or bad he was just going to keep doing it   blaming the Repubs? well, the thing is the Republicans have been pandering to these ugly parts of the country for a while. and i think that they, i think that they didn't condemn him enough   they all got to this point where they were, ok, well, i guess this guy is it, and they just jumped on his boat   so in a lot of ways, like, Trump read the room. um, but the Republican Party has been shifting in this direction for a really long time. because they've been aiming to win without thinking about, you know, who they are alienating. there's like, a lot of minorities in the US – particularly middle-class minorities, who probably would have voted Republican if it weren't for, you know, all the racist stuff, that is buried in it. and so – and that's not to say that like, that's a good or bad thing, it's just that strategically. Hilary, for example, only cared about Muslims in the context of national security. she also tried to – not in the same way, but she tried to pander in so many different, weird ways. like, when she had that weird Latina thing. when she was like, 'i have hot sauce in my bag'. do you, though? do you? i don't feel like you do. and it's like ok, you've, you've identified that Beyonce fans are, you know. important well. i mean, he's like, he's like a sort of caricature of an evil capitalist. he doesn't like, you know, if you asked Ralph Steadman to invent him you couldn't get any more, slicked-back hair and everything. on the giant yacht with the models, i mean. he's a joke isn't he? i can't see how he kept his knighthood. that's the obvious thing.   only time in my entire life i've seen the whole of Parliament unanimously agree on something. Oliver Shah's book coming out was kind of, a bit of an event. cos there's stuff in there. i don't know how that's not. when you read it, when you read this kind of smoke and mirrors, this incredibly convoluted little set up, he's dipping into BHS. i don't know how that's even legal. i mean, you read the details of it, surely that is some serious fraud or something. when you sort of think, you know, i'd probably get nicked for claiming benefits and doing a four hour shift somewhere, cash in hand, and i'd probably end up in prison. if, that's within the laws of the land then the laws of the land need changing. it would cheer me up a lot to see him. just from a really, you know, childish, revenge-ish point of view. i would love to see him. i mean i always, in my teens i was a bit of an anarchist, i've always hated sort of, businessmen. i've always distrusted them and found them quite vile. but like i say, he's become a symbol of them all to me. he's like a totem, totem scumbag. that report he tried to suppress, sort of a financial report.

hopefully that's going to come out at some point. hopefully they are going to put the boot in again. i mean, that would be nice. but no, he's probably just going to sail off into the sunset on his yacht, isn't he? with Kate Moss or something i thought Farage was great. i thought he was great. i think, i think he won the Referendum because he's got the common touch. he's eloquent. he's, he's funny, i think, as well. he's charismatic, and he's got, he doesn't care what people think of him. he's great in a debate. whereas, er, some of the, the Leave   Cameron, look, Cameron was a bloody good prime minister   he's charismatic, great on TV, JFK effect – ok, not as good looking. has a JFK effect, ok, and housewives dig him, right? sorry to be sexist but it's true. right

but what i'm saying is that, er. Cameron was fantastic up until the Referendum. he bottled it. in my opinion when he went to get the negotiation, negotiations. to me, i thought you're weak. you've lost this. he, he was arrogant, thinking, ah everybody will vote Remain, it'll be fine   i think what the Conservative party need, is, a Barack Obama type-figure. but not a bloody toff. and unfortunately, that's what it has come down to, now, which is identity politics   it needs somebody who has rational arguments, who has a common touch, that connects with the people funny like, now i can't remember the things that made me really excited. but, i think he was saying he wanted a kinder politics. and he seemed very involved in like, personal cases of, i can't remember where his constituency is. but, you know, that kind of thing. and he was saying we need a different way in politics. and when he was talking about nuclear weapons as well, saying that he would never press the button. and was like, that's a really strong stance to take. and also a lot of people agree that they don't want a nuclear war, but they'd still vote for a politician that said they would do it because it's kind of just what you do. but things are obviously not working, so we need to take drastic measures. and to say you're not going to bomb everyone with nuclear bombs seems drastic, but, but it shouldn't, shouldn't be a crazy thing to say. you know, it made a lot of sense.

for all, for all that everyone says, it's a disaster and he's quite out there. i don't think he's really out there. he just has the opinions of most people that i know   he was saying honest things, whereas politicians normally don't answer those kinds of questions. like, i don't, i've not heard another politician talk about saying they *would* bomb people with nuclear weapons, they would just say, well we need to invest in it. but that kind of thing gets annoying and i think people get fed up of it you can't put the toothpaste back in the tube. we've been free for two hundred years. we, we can't live under, that sort of European socialism model. it wouldn't work, it just wouldn't work. i mean a certain degree of socialism works if everyone agrees, and if you *really* check your government. regularly, often, and enthusiastically. then it can sort of work   but not here   William F Buckley, who is a hero, said, he said, 'i would trust the first fifty names in the Boston phonebook,' (cos he was from Boston) 'over our Congress.' just gimme a bricklayer. give me somebody who drives a bus, give me regular people who are in touch. i think that 'in touch', i think that's the thing. that people think with Trump, with all of his ridiculous, kind of, the drunk uncle at the bbq personality, he really is in touch. and he loves this country, he wants what's best for it. and he doesn't think that we are – terrible, a country, as Obama, Clinton did. so, he was kind of the soft option. i think that people said, you know what, i can deal with the goofiness because, he's not part of the system. i think there's a real, palpable feeling in this country, that career politicians, and these people that just live these lavish lifestyles, and have never signed the front of a paycheck, but only signed the back. there's just – we're tired of it. this was not how it was intended. you know, when the country first started, it was mostly wealthy landowners, and they went into politics sort of, almost like one does jury duty. like, it was the right thing to do and, i love this country so, i will stop making lots and lots of money for a few years and try to help steer this country in a good direction. and i don't think it was ever supposed to be for people who graduated law school, immediately started – ugggh. our congress has, like, two CPAs – two certified public accountants. everybody else is a lawyer, or something similar. yuck!

you know, all this silly stuff, i suppose it's silly, but for some people it's quite heartfelt, about this shape and size of bananas. i think in metrics, well, kilograms isn't it. these 'bloody imperial, right-wing, ancient, stones and pounds! what are you talking about'. but, er, the sovereignty thing. i quite like the European Court of Human Rights, and the European Supreme Court. i do like that. i do like the fact that, for example, the European Union, and this is a slight tangent, has got, and this is anecdotal of course. they outlawed cheaper car insurance for women, i love that. because, so sexist! the European Union brought parity. and it's done a lot of good. it really has. and in terms of the sovereignty, i don't trust British lawmakers, because they are from, made up from Oxbridge, and you know, a privileged elite. that's not, most of those people didn't get where they are on merit. they got there on birthright. whereas with the European Union, i think actually there is more of a chance to have a merit, meritocratic society. i really do believe that. i do i think we were talking about people on benefits. so, i think my position is quite, not unusual really, but some people are surprised because, i work in advertising and i live in London. i grew up on a council estate, and my mum's a teacher and she has a nice house now   but my dad's always been on benefits and unemployed and part of my belief in, in being socialist is, because when i was little, my mum went back to university to do a degree and to be a teacher. and she got grants to do that. and i'm like, there's no way mum could have done that. so that i don't. so we were talking about benefit cheats or something, not in a really serious way but the woman at work was like, oh, but it does encourage people not to work   it's very different being in London being like, why can't people go out and get a bar job, because there's hundreds of bar jobs. but up north, if you're not trained in the service industry which like, any of my friends, if we got unemployed we'd go and work in a sandwich shop and we'd be really good at it. but my dad can't, like, he's not, he can't give customer service or make sandwiches for people   i'm like, well, if it wasn't for Labour, i don't know if i would be here, because my mum wouldn't have been able to go to uni, she wouldn't have been able to become a teacher. we wouldn't have moved house from where we were living where all the schools were really bad. so i'm just very, i'm very aware i don't think i'd be where i am if life had been a bit different. whereas, a lot of people are like, doesn't matter what conditions you have, doesn't matter where you live, if you work hard   and i don't think that's true. because i'm not a particularly hard worker. i don't think i would've like, done anything, if I'd gone to a crap school. not everyone can be an exceptional genius and fight against adversity

BHS was, it was like the sort of infallible part of their lives. they'd all been in there since kids, since they were children. and, i just think they sort of. i don't know, maybe they didn't want to believe it. i don't know. a lot of those, a lot of it was, they were just very nice, trusting people. and they would assume, if your manager gets up and tells the staff, he wouldn't lie to you. because they themselves, they just assume everyone works on the same sort of moral code as them. people are trusting because they don't realise, how, you know, duplicitous managers can be   i thought i'd just have a bit of time. spend, you know, get through me redundancy pay and all that and then i'll start looking for work. and er, and then when i started looking for work, i couldn't get a single thing. i was applying online for a lot. exactly the same job i had done at BHS but at other shops. and there was, i'd get straight away refused, you know, you do the online questionnaires that sort of stuff. saying i wasn't suitable for doing, for doing the job i had just done for eight years perfectly well. i mean i was always getting praised by management that i was hard-working   and i was applying for things and they wouldn't even acknowledge that i'd applied. i was sort of like, got nothing for months. i think i was unemployed for 8 months. and then, yeah, i was on universal credit. you have to, i was sort of under the threat of sanctions and i had to go in for an hour every day and prove that i was applying for x amount of jobs a day, you know. you have to kind of earn your universal credit. and now that's all tied in with your rent as well, so if you don't do it right, it's not just that you don't have your spending money, your food money, your home is – you know what i mean?

in October i went to Keos, another island, and Mytilene in Lesvos and ninety percent of people who i met arrived from the areas where ISIS was occupying. they were in a siege like a circle like this. ISIS sieging them from here, and Assad closing the circle here, Assad forces. then two months ago, ISIS collapsed here, and Assad and Iranian forces came here instead, and the Russians started bombing in the air, yeah? they said the brutality of the Iranian-Assad forces were much worse than ISIS. they said ISIS, they – i mean not praising them, they said they were horrible, fierce, brutal. but then when the government come in you see this barbaric approach. because this siege collapsed, they were able to escape from here and escape to Turkey and Greece. these guys were under siege for three years. no food, no proper drink, no proper water, no proper thing. bombardment from the Americans, bombardment from the English, bombardment from the Russians. everybody was bombing them. and they come there to Moria and then live in this condition? you go out, and you start hitting your head against something what, the very end? it was like, it was bit like post-apocalyptic. kind of Walking Dead without the zombies. although i mean, some of the customers [*laughs*] no, i mean, it was grim. i wasn't there on the very last day, my very last day was on the day before. oh actually, there was the last day that i worked there when the shop was open. then we had to go in on the Sunday for some reason. was it Sunday or the Monday? and the shop was shut. and there was nothing to do. but we were told we had to come in and do eight hours, or something. everyone. mandatory. before the leaving drinks. and, er, we found a football. i was just kicking a football, i spent eight hours kicking a football around Tunbridge Wells BHS. because you know they'd sold the fixtures and everything. so it was just this big vast empty space. and yeah, that was my last, my last day in BHS was just booting a football around.

and then we all went and got hammered.
and er, the manager asked me outside for a fight. me and managers, i don't know what it is. he was an unpleasant fellow. the last manager was like a real idiot. leaving drinks – this probably should have been off the record. leaving drinks, i don't know, they were given two thousand pounds to buy everyone drinks. and er, he, he put that in his pocket. and any female, nice female, he'd be like, you can't have a drink until you've shown us your tits. he was one of these kind of geezers. and he was like, a terrible racist as well. just the most horrible bloke i've ever met

i remember saying to a friend of mine – a Labour friend of mine – that if Corbyn won the leadership election, i better start learning German because we might lose   because he would take the Labour Party out of the game, which is what he did. and we needed. if we'd had full Labour support, thirty percent of the Tory vote was needed to win. as it was, we got forty percent of the Tory vote. we beat expectations on the Tory side, but it wasn't enough   i was leafleting and going out canvassing and getting extremely wet. then the polls came in and i thought, well, ok. this seems OK. they conceded because the polls were all showing   they got the turnouts wrong. we were in the Blue Boar where we had our campaign headquarters. and at the beginning it was all very buzzing. George Osborne was there, and loads of people were there, and then gradually people started to drift away. and the results started coming in, and people got more and more depressed   i hadn't had any sleep in about two months. i remember walking up Primrose Hill,   there was a couple of people behind me going, oh look, there's the City of London with smoke coming out of it. i remember having quite a lot of conversations that were sort of like that week after 9/11 when everyone was talking about politics. and i also remember feeling that   this is that moment where everything looks OK, but it's a very thin layer of glass   and it's going to shatter it was, you know, lately, it has really hit me. i sort of, i just sort of plodded on for two years. i went to Homebase, didn't really make, like, great friends. i mean, i didn't, i didn't not get on with people.   i sort of. but then for some reason, a couple of weeks ago, it's just really hit me how much i miss some of the people. because i used to have a sort of, little gang, as often happens in work and that. it just worked out at BHS because i found people i liked, i had so many good laughs at BHS, i think i said, there are times i can genuinely remember laughing so hard i thought i was going to puke. because i was just begging people, everybody calm down because i am going to throw up. it was just, we were doing that all the time.

suddenly sort of remembering what a great time of my life that was.   and yeah, it's really grim. i started messaging some of them out of the blue and i think they just sort of thought   i was in my cups a bit, you know, and i was, 'i really miss folding towels with you.' it was a bit, you know. it was all, i might have come across a bit self-pitying. but genuinely, it has been grim though, losing touch. like suddenly, people you see every single day. it does become like, you know, your life, sort of thing. other than that i was down on the allotment talking to my chilli plants. so yeah, they were kind of my human companions. if i could have just done that forever. spend the day on the allotment growing my chilis and aubergines and what have you. and then, afternoon, just laughing my head off. . . like, it was like a little family. i know it's a dreadful cliché but it was, it was like a little family. so yeah, it has been pretty grim the most difficult thing is when you go to Moria camp you bring, for example, two hundred milk cans or three hundred depending on people like you to give me some help. and then i go out and i sit down on this rock in front of them, and i feel   it's like you had this little stone in the sea. you can't do anything. and then also being a father, for little children, this is a most difficult thing. seeing these children sleeping on the mud. have no milk, nothing. and i come back and see my daughters here. i met twelve year old children from Syria. none of them have been to school, ever. in Syria you go to school when you're six. and when you're six, started the war, and now it's seven years, you're like twelve or thirteen. so i asked them: have you been to school? no. never. imagine this. even if they go to Germany and learn, blah blah. but they still lost this period of their lives. like, my daughter now goes and has play dates. they missed it. they don't know how to write. and these guys, they will not ever write Arabic, for their own language. because if, *if*, they arrive in Europe, now they will learn a new language. and then this is the frustration, but also the anger. i just feel so angry. i feel, i want to bite somebody, for example. like physically, just go to some prime minster and just bite them. i feel so angry everything brushes, climate change brushes everything. and that's the problem. and that's the excitement. you know, you're talking about economics, you're talking about people being displaced, refugees, trying to build farming. all of it is being affected by climate. a guy, an English philosopher, he's actually in Texas. but came up with this notion of hyper objects. and a hyper object is something that is too big for human understanding. and big hyper objects for example, are nuclear Armageddon. you know, we had in the fifties, it was we suddenly realised that we had this capability to blow ourselves all up. what the hell does that mean? and then the other big one is climate change. there is no such thing as a climate refugee, though. climate is not recognised as a status being a refugee. the reason they won't do it is, i mean they won't give them refugee status is, there are going to be millions, hundreds of millions. i mean that's my beef about, everyone talks about climate as something that is going to be, three degrees rise, fifty years. it means nothing to people. but if i sort of said, oh, if we get three degrees rise then probably it means a hundred million climate refugees knocking on Europe's door. which is what will happen. and they go, oh shit. that is a problem. we've got to reframe the language. we, we really do. you see people who. you feel that threatened you will do anything to try and survive somewhere else. and also, where is our, where is our capacity, for being human? you know? i mean especially in this country. it is bonkers in the beginning it was kind of a collection point. sleep there, you could stay over. the people were, until the terrible Turkey-EU deal in March, the people were very friendly. but then after March 2016 Moria became the prison. if you go now to Moria – i'll send you a picture – they write out big, 'welcome to Moria Camp' and somebody crossed it and said 'prison'. it is now, i mean   it's one of the most depressing places i've been in my life. it is, it's where you don't have any feeling, any humanity, any dignity, any safety, any security. you have only one thing: it's called humiliation. they have been, some people have been there more than a year now. mostly bad. we all speak of men and the kind of bad things they might do in their lives. but single young men are really badly treated there. if you are a woman and you bring a baby, you have hope to leave. if you are older, you have hope to leave. but the EU, the EU control everything in Moria – like the asylum process, everything.   and mostly everybody is refused. Syrians are just still counting to ten before they send them back to Turkey. they are sending people, but secretly, discreetly. i mean, if you are about to be removed, they take you to prison. or if you make a problem, like fight or something. a very young Syrian guy who was detained there, told me things like what's happening in the prison. he said it's exactly the conditions in Syria before and during the war even. and it's torture. i mean they beat people. i've never seen. through my work with Amnesty i went to prisons in the Middle East, visited prisons and saw prison conditions. this is the worst i've ever seen. i went to Yemeni prisons, even detention centres. i've never seen the desperation like Moria. they   from Syria, i interviewed last month, i mean i spoke to and documented some. they said, 'we wished we'd stayed under the bombs' it was a very, very – weird day. i'd taken the day off but of course i was on my bloody laptop. and, just as i was literally about to close my laptop, er, an email came through from a colleague saying, i'm not sure you've seen this: forward – Jo Cox MP attacked. and i was like, what? and i went on the BBC. and i was like, skim reading, heart-rate up and i was like   something's gone on, something's gone on. and i skim read. and in my head at first, the first reports were really confused. and it almost sounded like, in my head at least, probably to protect myself, there was like, her, in her surgery. so, 'gunshots outside Jo Cox's surgery' i thought well she's inside, and there's some commotion on the street, by coincidence. and then i read more, then i read more. and i'm churning through all this crap on the internet. and this one said: 'she's been shot.' fuck she's been shot. fucking hell, she's been shot. well it could be an arm or a leg. and you know, if you're shot you're. i imagine if someone's shot, i don't know, you don't imagine that it's close range, or i didn't. and then i read that report that just stopped me in my tracks that said she's been stabbed. i thought hang on a minute, she's been stabbed. the guy's right here. and he's got a gun. she's been shot from here. oh my god   and the fucking phone didn't work. the fucking phone didn't work. it was a really hot day. you know sometimes like the mugginess, or the hotness, the mugginess sort of messes with the signal?   there's all these reports. and my phone, i'm answering it and it doesn't work   'how is she?' – she's not going to make it. and i thought, don't fucking say a word. don't fucking say a word. don't say, are you sure? don't. just don't say anything. and i hung up. and i just collapsed. and wailed. like a kind of, like a sort of medieval. like, just wailed

when i was in Keos – this is one of the worst
things i've ever seen. somebody hanged himself. he
survived. he didn't die. the camp is an old factory,
empty, abandoned. so he went up and jumped with
a thing around him, with a rope around his neck.
eighteen years old.   luckily there were some
people who went up immediately and cut the rope.
so he fell on the floor. i don't know what happened
to him, but he was unconscious. he didn't die, for
sure, i know that. but imagine if you are eighteen
WHY? why i'm here? you know what i mean. it's
the EU and Germany created a culture of despair
that, literally, they drive you to the edge, and you
call your neighbour or brother in Syria, and you say
don't come. it's the idea, and ninety percent of people
i spoke to, they believe that they are torturing them
– let's say not torturing them – tormenting them
because   *To make people not come?*   exactly

and everyone's rallying. Jo's strong. [*bangs table*]. she's going to make it. [*bangs table*]. she's going to be alright. i didn't want to believe it   it was becoming, like, national news. you know, she's in Leeds hospital. she's been airlifted. and all the channels were, it was like. it was like one of them moments. and then and he said: they just announced that she died. and then i just. and, so. it was just the most fucking, fucked up day. ever i was waiting on the land, on the beach. i also took people from the water. there are different feelings. also there's big, terrible issues by the smugglers, like imposed by the smugglers. like, you take a boat, and they give you a knife, like very sharp knife, and they say, 'the moment you reach the beach, the shores, you stab the boat. because otherwise the police will gut you and send you back.' and you know, it's a rubber boat. when i came, people were all doing this – stabbing the boats – sometimes because they were terrified because of the journey and terrified of the unknown. like, what's waiting for them? and they stab the boats inside the water and people went in the water. then i developed – literally i was the only Arabic speaker that time on this piece of the Eftalou beaches.   i started this scheme, told it to every single European in Arabic: 'don't stab the boats! nobody will send you back.' that's a poem, actually. and then everybody could see the Spanish, English, blah blah blah: 'don't stab the boat!' in very   English Arabic

أمان

so, the most important thing – the word is called 'aman'. aman is safety, and aman it works in Arabic and Farsi, same word. and Swahili. so people who came from Africa, they also understand it no. no. didn't, i mean. i think i read one article, i thought, you shouldn't have fucking read that. you know, i was interested in her   what, what actually happened. was she alright – how much pain was she in? what. you know, how, how much did she suffer? and i read one thing about the details, and i was like, i just shouldn't have read that. because. yeah   we went into this organisation-mode that just, you know. she existed around an entire network of campaigners and people that worked on issues. and someone was like, right, we're going to make some fucking good come out of this in her memory. i was like, fucking bring it on, what we doing? and it was just a really weird way of channelling everyone's, like, mad energy   there we were, having a fucking conference call on Friday morning. and again – it was the day after but it felt like every hour, or every bit of time felt like, it was quick and slow at the same time. it was really strange. we wanted to bring some light out of the darkness. and, and raise some money for good causes, and not let the dark stuff win, and not let the guy who killed her be all over the papers. but have her and her life define her legacy, not her death

yes, so there was that. and then
bloody Prince died! and then
George Michael died! and then
everyone died! yes. we all
watched Top of the Pops. i did
read up on it. what is this
phenomenon of everybody
dropping dead at the same time,
it seems? there was an analysis
saying that if you go back to the
forties or fifties, whatever, there
were relatively few stars
compared to. and then the
number of stars has kind of
grown. and of course the ones
that we all share, as you say, at
that particular age

it was my birthday treat in 1977 when it came out. i fell asleep. we were eating jam doughnuts and i fell asleep as soon as the credits started and i slept through the whole thing. so the first time i suppose was Hannah and Her Sisters. they formed the Stanislavski Catering Company because they were both out-of-work actresses and i was sitting there going   i think i grew up wanting to be an out-of-work actress. i don't think i grew up wanting to be an actress. i grew up wanting to be an out-of-work actress who got funny jobs and hung around with funny people   that's all i've done all my life. that's what i do. i have closer relationships with people on film than i do with real people, which is a bit of a worry. but i do have   which is why when they die it gets really upsetting because most of these people i've watched on film since i was a kid, and i do feel i have a stronger relationship with them. which is why i usually want to sleep with actors because i feel like i've known them longer than i've known real people. and that's why it always never works. it's ridiculous. it falls apart because i don't trust the civilians

stay up. that was literally   stay in the
Premiership. i remember, even though we had
had The Great Escape, we had had those eight
matches   The Independent said, ha: 'strong
candidates for relegation.' and i thought it was
a good side but i thought it lacked touches of
skill, really. for a premiership team, that ability
to pass the ball around   i thought it lacked a
bit of ability. i thought, you know, i thought
they probably would stay up. i thought they
probably would stay up. but i didn't think
they'd finish in the top half   if you were a
member of the supporters' club you could go
in the supporters' club area   a small area
behind one of the goals. and er, at the back of
it, there was actually a bar   and even after the
ban on alcohol, you could actually buy a drink.
you were, i don't think you were allowed to
take it to the seats, but you could go to this little
bar and buy a drink. and it was only a few, you
know it was a tiny, proper little bar with seats!
it was like a little pub room at the back of the
terraces. and then next to it was the sort of tea
room with the prices still chalked up on a
blackboard. you know, it was a sort of, thirty-
three p for a cup of tea. served by a lady who
had obviously been serving it for thirty years in
a pinny. everything you could want from a
traditional football club

we did watch Top of the Pops. in my house, we watched Top of the Pops. so i probably would have seen it. you know, i was a punk by the time i was sort of thirteen, fourteen. i never saw the Sex Pistols, sadly. but i was quite naughty. and i just used to go on my own. but because i'd met people, they would kind of look after me. i didn't realise it at the time that i had older punks who would keep an eye on me because they knew i was young   it's like, one of the big things about being a fan and listening to music, it's the other people who love them too. so my friend Claudia, Claudia Krupwell, bless her. was probably the friend who i, first kind of, had adoration sessions with. you know, you can be together in company and in shared adoration of something. and sit and play a whole album and barely speak! but sing a-long, and, you know, just   just enjoy it. and just love it. and play album after album and just probably quite similar to a lot of other, um, middle-ranking clubs. not big money clubs, they're not top six clubs. but they are clubs nonetheless who have a long tradition where the supporters have to put up with failure as much as success. sometimes more failure than success. somehow, it's rough with the smooth, sticking with them, type feeling. it's your club, the one you go to see. you moan about them, but you still follow them. and i think there's a bit of a, a togetherness about it. we're in it together   and you know, the reaction of the crowd. it was a crowd that pushed them on to that victory. and something different was happening, you know.   that Aston Villa game, i just remember it because the atmosphere was fantastic, you know, and thinking if that atmosphere can keep going in the club then yeah, we'll do alright   very little negativity from the fans. and so there was a strong ability, there was a feeling, sort of starting to grow between the fans and players. which somehow you could sense. a lack of groaning and moaning from the supporters. often shouting different players names. keeping going with the singing and shouting, even though they were down, you know, perhaps one nil down. and applauding the players off the pitch even after a draw, or a loss very. yeah. like, the Yorkshire roots and the people. i could relate to so many things about her, that she was interested in, Labour politics, she was interested in anti-poverty fight and the development world everything had sort of fallen into place, really. she was working on women. she was working on Syria. she was very used to understanding what the issues were in conflict situations and all of that. so i think when Syria came along and it was such a devastating crisis, she kind of took that on and she was very determined to, to do as she'd always done. it's about doing what's best for the people on the ground, it's like, party politics, shouldn't really come into it. you shouldn't really be politicking with it. so, she would, famously, always try and get cross-party support, get things done that way. but she was really really, a homebody as well. and that, that's exactly what i was. and i always felt like, oh, i'm a bit in-between places. and, i don't, you know, i've always felt like, a foot here and a foot there. and here was someone who seemed to have the same interests. pursuing those things, and also that very strong connection to home. she didn't want to be *an* MP. She wanted to be an MP for home. where she'd come from, Batley and Spen

as an actor, i always saw myself as
a best friend. i grew up watching
screwball comedies where there were
always strong female figures, but i
always fancied being the best friend of
the strong female character. i was
always the secretary with the smart
line and get off quickly. i was never
going to be front stage. i did this play
and i went for the part of the maid. it
was called Minna von Barnhelm. it
was an 18th-century German comedy
– they don't come around very often.
and it was about a gentlewoman and
her maid and she falls in love with
an officer and there are other officers
and it's   for the four people who
saw it, they all liked it very much. but,
i   i auditioned for it, and i didn't get
the maid. they gave me the main part.
so i was Minna von Barnhelm! and
she was the romantic   she got to
fall in love and this was not what i
expected at all. i suddenly had to stand
there and just do it straight and be
sincere. no! no! this isn't supposed to
be happening. you're not supposed to
be   looking at me like that because
that's not who i am. i'm   i'm the
maid! i'm the woman in the corner
making the jokes. i'm Eve Arden. i'm
Carrie Fisher. it's very strange

i don't identify with any of his characters like that.
no. that's quite a surprising question, in a way. i'm
sure that some people do. but. no   i never
identified with being him   but it's weird as well.
i've had this thing the past couple of years that
actually he's just a normal bloke. like anyone is. he,
whereas previously i just thought he was so
extraordinarily different from any other human that
i could ever look at. and because i found such joy and
pleasure in looking at his face. it really was different
to me. that, and because that whole thing of being a
space man and an alien as well, like that. he seems
utterly otherworldly to me. and i've more come to
the realisation recently   and i suppose him ageing
as well. blimey, wow. he's actually just a bloke. and
like if he hadn't been David Bowie, he'd have just
been David Jones and, you know. done something
else   i love his teeth. that's the thing. i absolutely
adore his teeth. and i actually was a bit upset with
him when he had his teeth done. because these little
crooked teeth. these little crooked things. i find him
very very beautiful and, and, like other   i'm
bisexual, so   i do find him beautiful. absolutely.
he moves me physically. i am absolutely physically
moved. it's just different to the kind of lust that you
would have, just for a normal person that you would
lust after. that kind of lust and desire and physical
attraction is just separate. because it's him. it's just
that he's different to all other people. i know it
sounds mad but, i am, i am doing it for this interview,
but it's the truth. it's true. there's no other person
who i feel that way about

and then of course you see you go and see Postcards from the Edge, which she wrote. you get Shirley MacLaine playing Debbie Reynolds and it's glorious! there is an amazing scene – i've probably told you about this before that i think about most days when i put my makeup on. i've told you this. i might bore the hell out of you. *It's not on tape though.* it's not on tape. so Debbie Fisher who's played by the wonderful Shirley MacLaine is a survivor and is   she is Seventy-six Trombones! every time she opens the door. she is Singin' in the Rain! every day, and she runs a car into a tree one day and has this car crash, has to be taken to the hospital. and for the first time in the movie you see this woman without her wig on, with no makeup very small and fragile, looking quite elderly. and she's in this little hospital bed, and her daughter comes in and goes oh my god, and she's just   but there's photographers outside, there are newspaper men saying 'whatever's happened to this star?' so she pulls herself together. and all the time she's talking and i can't remember what she's talking about. but as she's talking she's putting herself back together. she takes her scarf and she wraps it around her head   she looks like a little plucked bird. she does it up in a turban which pulls her face back at the same time. she takes – she's got like, three pieces of makeup, and she puts a couple of swipes of blusher on. and then she does something magnificent with a couple of [*whooshing sounds*] across her eyelids. slash of lipstick, puts her fur coat on and then opens the door of the hospital room. and it's ta-da! and it's the armour. and she's done it. she can face it. she can do it. and the daughter hates her, but is also in complete admiration and she's, you know, might *kill* her at the end of the day. but she's managed to get out of the room like that. and, you know, i think it's a wonderful scene. absolutely wonderful scene. and I think a lot of straight women and gay men [*laughs*] feel that way first thing i did was phone Ria. is it true? because it was on Facebook. i phoned Ria. she said yes, it's true. i went to a friend. where did we go? we went to some gallery. or was it the British Museum or something? and we went and walked round. i was in the British Museum and i said, 'i'm sorry i have to go home. i can't cope.' i can't look at these things. i don't care! i don't care about anything! i have to go home and, and see what's going on. see what people are saying. and actually i remember finding social media, Facebook, really great and comforting. and looking at all this stuff. and dear friends of mine, who knew. who know, of my fandom. who were very loving and lovely, sending me messages and looking after me and stuff. and so i spent a lot of the day just looking at the screen, listening. putting headphones on and listening to the music. yes, i was absolutely in grief. and shock

it really really got me. and, and there'll never be anyone who dies from now on, who, who is a stranger, who will affect me as much as he did. because i can't – i haven't got the time, to grow as much, of a kind of, you know, a fan worship and hero worship thing   loving him as i have since being, really young. and also just because, cause he had this yearning to not die. as most people do. and in his album Black Star, you know, he obviously really had so much more to do and he wants to spend time with his daughter and his son and his wife, and carry on making music with just   like – really?! FUCK. what a bummer! dammit! i've got easily another twenty years to do stuff, you know. so that's, that's really, really   painful

when you say what were the great moments for me
to remember   the home game against Everton
that was, you know, just a big lovefest really, the
whole time. it was just a sea of colour. people were
just singing all through the match. you know, it was
just continuous. and then they had a big parade at the
start, a lot of fireworks. and then they had Andrea,
Bot – not Boticelli, Bocelli, who came out and sang.
it was – it was delirious   as we were walking down
– as i said, down through our lucky walk, i noticed
that there were, there were a crowd of supporters
with small rucksacks. who were all singing about
Claudio Ranieri. and they were singing very nicely!
you know, singing *in tune*. and i thought, hang on a
minute, what's going on here? are they Leicester
supporters? who are they? and i got talking to them
and they were from Italy. and they'd come over from
Italy   they didn't have tickets to get into the game.
i think they were hoping to see it on the big screen.
but there wasn't one, because Sky wouldn't allow it.
and they just went to the ground, and then into
Leicester. just to be in Leicester. and there were
hundreds of Italians. Ranieri fans. and i think also
they, they had come to appreciate Leicester's victory,
to celebrate it. they had come from Naples and
Rome! i said, 'where have you come from?' he said
'Naples. oh, we came on the bus. we came on the
coach.' it's just extraordinary. it's mad. and not even
going to see the game. just wanted to be in Leicester.
and shout Claudio Ranieri's name

and actually, we were talking about the Bowie night that i did, 'Let All the Children Boogie'. you remember? my memorial to him. and the funny thing about memorials, you do it to someone who's dead to honour, they don't give a shit – they're dead. but you still want to do these things to honour them. so it must be to do with you.   i wanted to honour him and honour my love for him, by committing myself that evening to really absorbing and concentrating. i didn't talk to anyone. and i think that's a quality of concentration, or an ability to be allowed to focus on something. it's really, it's hard to do that. a whole album? a whole song? dip, dip, dip, change, change, change, change, change, change. and i do do that as well now. the telly's on, i've got my laptop. i laugh at myself! the telly's on, i'm doing something with my laptop and i'm playing scrabble and i can't believe it! i've got three screens – how did it happen? and i would say, you know i've talked a lot about loss and grief and all of those things and it was his death that actually made me decide to pull my fucking finger out. i needed a deadline, i needed some peers. and a course of work to force me to do it. otherwise i just end up   uh, i haven't done it. oh, another year's gone by, oh shit! and another year's gone by, oh shit! and another year's gone by, oh shit! oh another year's gone by, oh shit! and i've died. you know, and i thought, i really have to intervene in this. because it really does all end. and, and his death, apart from all the things that are to do with him, really really [*makes sound of explosion*] did that to my brain. and i thought – no messing about we were just very lucky, very fortunate to have shared the time with her that we did. and what we would remember of Jo. what we loved about her. and how she was always smiley, and cuddly. happy, you know. and that was the thing. she was an MP for a year of her life but she was – which is really important and i've no doubt at all that she would have gone on to be a cabinet minister, whatever she wanted. the sky was the limit for her, because she had it all. she had brains, she had savvy. but she was also very human. and very, likeable. i think her legacy in particular on, her journey and who she was and, being that girl from Yorkshire charming people along the way and getting, getting shit done   that kind of supporting people, and women to achieve what they want to achieve. 'Jo would put her arm around you and pull you along as she gave you advice.' and that's exactly how it was. you always felt like she was pushing you forward – but with kindness. so i think that's a massive legacy   also Syria was a huge piece of work for her, and the community cohesion stuff, you know, trying to live that 'we have more in common than that which divides us' at a very local level. but also, she wasn't just these issues. she was really someone who made a lot of things happen because of who she was as a person and this whole era, age, age that we're stuck in right now will soon get displaced. here we are talking about climate change. it would have been very rare that somebody would have come to me twenty years ago and said 'let's talk about climate change.' i mean they did a survey recently, for people under, i think under thirty. and their most pressing concern, along with all the others, was climate change. oh it's fantastic! i mean, you know, i mean this is why, this is what stops me falling into despair. because, you know, it's like, oh my god, we're not making any progress. then you think, but wait a minute, in eighteen years, this subject is now at the forefront, especially among the younger people. it is their future, their inheritance. so if we can make that kind of progress in eighteen years, then you kind of go, well, the next eighteen years should deliver enormous change. except we're at the hard, you know, we're really at the coal face right now. thinking of how we live on this, how we live. i mean, it affects everything. one of my major reasons for staying in Europe is that we so need to work together, right across the whole planet, for something like climate change erm, i did have disagreements but, but not loads. i didn't say anything on twitter. i stayed out of, i don't like arguing with people online, i try to stay away. but, there's people. like, my boyfriend's family   i got into, not an argument, because i was being very polite, because it was his family friend, but er, the man. he was talking about, er, he was like oh i saw you on the telly. 'the man's an idiot'. and he was talking about immigration, and, 'it doesn't matter that all the young people are voting, the people who have got the money and who are in charge aren't voting for him'. and i was like yeah, but they'll all be dead. meaning him, obviously. so then i was like, oops. but i did mean it. you will be dead soon. all the whole generation will be dead   but then also, so that family friend that i had that argument with. he was talking about how Labour would run the country into the ground like, finance wise. it's weird. it's like the right-wing people think he's, doesn't know anything about finance and economics. and the left-wing people think that he's going to flood the country, and disarm all the bombs. but then, young people are voting for him. so, and young people are getting older, if you see what i mean. so i feel like it, it will, it will change

i mean, Trump is a lot like Uber. you know? he's
just like. he has like: i see this need, fuck the rules,
i'm just going to say it. and, you know, institution
be damned. you know, like Uber, you know Uber
is like, we're gonna, we're gonna change how
people take rides. and we don't give a fuck about,
taxi medallions, and all these people who make a
living in this way. we're going to, like, radically
undervalue the work that they do. i feel like it's
because he came through reality TV. i feel like he's
shameless. nothing sticks. and, like, you know, he,
he, he's learned to come through a pipeline where
all attention is good attention   i'm not sure yet.
i feel like, i feel like the Democrats so far, from
what it looks like, they, their approaches, it feels
like they are clinging to this centre thing and i just
don't think it's going to work. i feel like they tried
it with Hilary. i mean, some people say that
Bernie's going to run again. he's like, seventy-
seven. i don't, i think they. i dunno – old people
shouldn't run for president. i think this is the
problem: we're trying to address it in a Hollywood
way. Hollywood is like, 'let's make more remakes'
and it's like, no, just do something new. you need
something new

they, the Democrats and the liberals are better at optics. and, we, we Republicans find someone who wants his turn. whereas the democrats are like, ok, let's look at this – partially because Hollywood and the creative arts align themselves, they're really good at optics. they find people, like Obama, who are just likeable. and vote-able   we need to stop bringing Bushes to the party and they need to stop bringing Kennedys and Clintons to the party. people are ready for a change. they want someone like you. you know, someone who is bright and young, and has some ideas. you know, we need more people that don't see this as a really *really* lucrative career. we just need people who love the country if someone had really, with a passion for retail, had wanted to make that shop work. found out what people were coming in for. found out what BHS meant to people and catered to that and improved upon it. then yeah, i reckon it could still be going. i know retail, like i said, is meant to be in a bit of a crisis, but. maybe that's what's happening everywhere. maybe all these shops there's someone trying to squeeze everything and there's all these people getting richer and richer whilst the shops are selling cheaper and cheaper tat. and er, and the staff. you know, when you're sort of, on minimum wage and sort of being treated like crap then, you're not going to be offering good service. of course people would rather go online rather than have to come and talk to me. *you seem pretty nice.* yeah, but you're not asking me for advice on towels. i can be, i can be quite dismissive. i mean, to be honest i mean, we have the technology to deliver this change right now. um, we have the money to deliver it right now. we don't have the willpower to deliver it right now   the big one they're talking about is energy. you know, for the past two hundred years, we've been digging stuff up and burning it. now, we've found out that we don't need to do that. you know, that there's enough energy around from sun, from wind, from, you know, tidal powers. if we can harness that, then we can deliver it. the technologies are enough advanced, that if it was ramped up with huge sums of money, we would deliver it. you know, an example, a silly one, is putting solar roofs on English roofs is kind of crazy. but, you know, you've got the Sahara desert. if you put up a huge solar farm there and could ship that energy. pretty much like you go down there and dig the oil up. shift that and you could actually deliver the world's electricity. we can do that, we now have that technology, but what you've got to do is switch all the money from going into digging up oil and switch it into building those kinds of huge solar farms. corporations tend to, would rather die than change. i mean, that's part of their make-up.   the whole fossil fuel industry will, eventually, just shoot itself in the head. but, it has, you know, the amount of money they are spending, i think it's four trillion dollars over five, six years. give me that four trillion dollars and invest it in new technology. woof! we're off!

and that's when the Brussels move came on. i was very frustrated by actually an awful lot of Remainers in Britain, rather than Leavers   they couldn't accept that leaving the EU was somehow legitimate. they, and i guess if i had ended up with an English girlfriend or something i would've wanted Britain somehow to stay in by hook or by crook   it could start adapting. start reorienting the English economy away from those sectors that are dominated by regulated international trade. move it more into management consulting, more into   IT services, all kinds of things that don't need regulating and passporting. you have to accept that the legal sector is going to go down. you have to accept that finance is not going to be quite what it used to be and somehow you probably have to do something about immigration – i don't know what. if   if they want to do things that are a shock, they should start preparing for that shock. that's why they should've done the impact assessments. they could've done this. they could've said this is a moment of national independence and national renewal. let's all come together. it's going to be very difficult. but at the end of it we will have freedom and we will be able to start a new path for Britain, and it's going to be brilliant. and Remainers would've grumbled and said it was nonsense, but   enough of them would've got along with it oh not until. i think we all felt. i mean, it was only when we started to build a substantial lead that we thought it was possible. you know they were taken to pieces by Arsenal five two early on in the season. and everybody thought ohh. well, that's one of the big boys we're playing now. and maybe, you know, let's not get our hopes up too much, because once we start playing the top six teams, this is what's going to happen. Theo Walcott   Sanchez scoring a hat trick. they looked, they looked a different class and they were really, in a way. you know, they were a real class act. but it wasn't, the whole thing, it wasn't just about class, that season. i mean, you have to remember Gary Lineker, with the famous underpants thing. and there were all the other commentators saying, round about Christmas time, well you know Leicester have done well, but it's time they went back to where they belong, sort of mid-table. they were all fairly sort of disbelieving   even right up until the end, really. when Tottenham were chasing them Vardy sent off. could they do it without Vardy? i think it was Danny Murphy, no not Danny Murphy. somebody else on Match of the Day said, well Tottenham will be licking their lips now. so right up until then, i think we all felt, oh dear. because

          and Tottenham are a very good side. and Leicester are just, maybe faltering. will they, will they have the strength of character to go over the finishing line? and of course, of course they did. i think, i think a lot of clubs and football supporters picked up on it as being, it is, it can be done. it's extraordinary, it is unusual, but you don't need to give up. if you've got the right players, the right manager, the right supporters, the right club, the right atmosphere in the club. it can happen. it won't happen often. but it can happen

i'm contradicting myself,
hugely. if I had a chance
to vote against the British
establishment, i would've
done. i just want to give
everyone a bloody nose.
do you know what i
mean? but i saw that the
European Union was an
establishment as well. an
evil empire. i had a shot
of whisky and voted
Leave. it's a hypothesis. a
hypothesis. we'll be
alright. we will be alright.
yeah, we'll still be able to
buy a coffee, we'll still be
able to watch Match of
the Day. buy a house. we
will evolve and adapt.
whether it's good or bad

that said, one of the things that i'm pretty convinced about is, we have to change in a very short, globally, we have to change in a very short timeframe. and that cannot be a rational change. you cannot design it. it, it, it's too large a scale to politically manoeuvre. so, in history, cultural shifts have happened in incredibly short periods of time. even in recent history, some of them have been horrendous, like the birth of Nazism, which was eventually a cultural shift. but then you also had the sixties and you had that whole coming out of, you know that amazing sense of optimism that came basically through music and poetry. and painting, and Rauschenberg, oof, huge.

it just came out of nowhere. and everybody went wow, this is exciting, this is different. and we want that. and, you know, the computer age, the whole internet basically was another cultural change. um, so being creative can, that's what will happen. i mean, somehow. at some point in the near future, we will just decide, that actually, there is a much better world to create out there than the one, the one we're stuck with i think she is right. but we make it damn hard for ourselves to see it sometimes   obviously it was a core part of her speech and something that people have picked up on. and it sort of resonates with people because we are in a very divided country in many ways. but, what that shouldn't do, that phrase, is mask the fact that Jo was supremely political. and had political positions. and had positions that she fought for. so yeah, she would try and get things done in the spirit of building coalitions and working with people. but it didn't mean that she didn't have strong positions. i think that can sometimes be a confusion. that it means 'oh, don't have a position, let's just all come together kum ba ya.' no, not at all. we have to fight for what we believe in. and you know, put your case. and let's work with as many people as possible to do that

i had started going, after   as a
goodbye present the receptionists,
staff bought me an entertainment
package at Leicester City. and we sat
at a table with some Leicester City,
with some die-hard Leicester City
fans, and chatting to them   and she
said it was amazing, how loyal they
are, going to all the away matches. she
said, it's incredible how much it
consumes of their life. and then i said,
well, why don't we get a season ticket?
so we got a season ticket. and they
looked like they were going down. and
it came up to renew the season ticket.
and i said, 'do we want? shall we
renew?' this has always been my thing
about football, is, it doesn't –
obviously it would be great to be at
the top level, but it doesn't have to be.
so i said yeah, no, let's renew. and then
of course, a week later, The Great
Escape starts   it put Leicester on the
map. undoubtedly, worldwide. in fact,
the Richard III thing as well. you
know, that was all coming out at the
same time. and in fact, at the last
match, the Everton match. they had a
plane flying over the stadium with one
of those banners. and it, the banner
said: 'i knew you'd do it' – Richard III'

what's work? what's success in therapy? would she have been worse if she hadn't been having it? is it like the Tory-Liberal Democrat coalition? 'yes, that was terrible, but think about how much worse it would've been if the Tories had been on their own!' did thirty-eight years of therapy turn her into a viable person? i don't know. and yet she said that people would say, 'the tragic life of Carrie Fisher' and that she refused to believe that – it's not tragic at all. absolutely not   she wanted to rely on her wit rather than her looks. and she was extremely funny. and, even though – it sounds weird – but even though she died at the age of sixty, she did survive. which was admirable. she was a ballsy woman. *if you could only save one Carrie Fisher film, what would it be?* Spaceballs 2 [*laughs*] no, it would have to be When Harry Met Sally. her and Bruno Kirby are both dead now. and they're in bed. and it's the greatest, the greatest romantic line ever. because it's about marriage. it's about   breathing. it's not about the height of passion. it's about   they each take a phone call from Harry and Sally. so Harry calls Jess up and says, 'my god i've just slept with Sally.' at the same time, in the same bed Marie takes a call from Sally, and Sally says, 'i've just slept with Harry.' so they're both leaning over the sides of their beds having these phone conversations going, 'oh we're so happy for you! should've happened years ago. no? it didn't go well? oh it's ok.' and they both put their phones down. and then they look at each other. and she looks at him and says, 'tell me i never have to go out there again.' and he puts his arm around her and says, 'you never have to go out there again.' and it's beautiful! two lovely ordinary-looking people have found each other and it's absolutely glorious. it's great the best thing about it? there's lots of happy stories. actually there is a fantastic sense of determination among people. i met this family when the border closed in March 2016. i fell in love with their little girl called Lin. came and grabbed my leg and completely stuck to me   and they had the Family Reunion, but imagine, Lin, Ghaith and Abdul, three children were waiting for their dad for eighteen months, sorry, for twenty months. he was in Germany with the little brother. these three, during their stay in the camp, they learned fluent German and fluent English from their mobile. from their mobile. like, these guys became the star of the camp, translating, speaking to people. and also they came from a very conservative family   this Ghaith, last time i met, he was talking to me telling me about human rights, LGBT. imagine! fourteen from Idlib! the most conservative place in Syria. and he went to Germany, and he came to school and the teacher told him: 'but i just thought, you just came?' and Ghaith said to him, 'yeah' – but in German! and she said, 'but you speak fluent German? two days later the social worker came and said, 'where did you learn your German?' and the three of them said, 'in the caravan.' they arrived when they're like thirteen, eleven and nine, and they travelled together, just the three of them, and they left eleven, thirteen and fifteen. Ghaith, like he's on my Facebook. he comments on my English posts in English. he didn't learn how to speak. he learned how to write. the other day when i met this gay man   Ghaith – he's fourteen now – and he said to me, he wrote to me, 'everybody has the right to choose what they want to be in life.' in his area in Syria this gay man would be killed. and like, i was like crying. i literally cried. fluent in English. fluent in German. amazing communication skills. and in the camp you have two options: you have two options: you can go to violence or despair, blah blah, or you go to the other side. so many people, so many children, are doing the other story, the good story, like learning on their own. another girl told me, i said to her 'what do you want? usually i don't buy people mobiles.' and she said, 'i just want to communicate in my life,' so i bought her a mobile well, it's part of it is, i'd rather live like this. you know, i'm having a ball. i mean, it's a struggle, but i'm still having. i mean i work with some extraordinary people we talk about some extraordinary things. and i'd rather be optimistic. i mean, it doesn't matter two beans to anybody or history whether i am optimistic or pessimistic, so i'd much rather choose to be optimistic   i mean [*laughs*] we are a very unpredictable animal. we really are. you look at the value of art and writing, like War and Peace, you know, it just wraps up how complicated human beings are. so, we will be unpredictable. but, there's our excitement. we are an amazing animal i try not to rage these days. i'm too old for raging. no, i do go through. i do have moments, you have moments where you sit and dwell on it all and think about. that's what i was doing when i was texting all my friends drunkenly, going, 'i really miss you'. so i try not to do that too much. i don't think it's healthy. like you say, you just got to see the funny side. all the way   i just thought, i'm going to try and make the most of this. i'm in the middle of something. somebody drove a bulldozer through my life and i was either going to sit there in the rubble crying for the rest of my life, or just think: well this is happening, what fun stuff can i do? and you see now i get to come to London and hang out with a poet. you don't get to do that every day, do you? i just think, oh well sunshine. energy. fizz. sparkle. er, like, just, hilarious. fun. er, amazing chats about everything from politics to, you know, the usual stuff that female friends talk about. to family, to juggling it all when, you know, succeeding and failing, and, all of that. and just, like a woman who, just was so warm and exuded friendship and generosity, in a way that just, made you feel like, just. you could be with her endlessly *this is great. i can press stop?* i think it's time for another song.

go on then, play me one more song

... What are we coming to/no room for me, no fun for you/I think about a world to come/Where the books were found by the Golden ones/Written in pain, written in awe/By a puzzled man who questioned/What we were here for/All the strangers came today And it looks as though they're here to stay

'oh you pretty things, don't you know you're driving your mamas and papas insane.' you know – what are you? and it's like, well, i'm just me! just something that i noted down: a really weird thing about being sad at the same time as being happy. and i'm really interested in that, it's such a weird one. but remembering a loved one who is lost, just thinking about my dad for example. you feel so desperately sad. at exactly the same time as feeling really happy in a memory. how can you have both? you really can have both. at the same time, not one and then the other. and with Bowie. very very sad. and i still get really sad, about him dying. i do really feel sad some days. and then you know, the pleasure, of everything that he did. having all his work and the pleasure of everything that he did. it's undoubtedly sad. because he didn't want to die. that's what makes it sad. you know, where the fuck did Monday go? it's all too quick i'm just grateful for the opportunity to share my faith and my perspe ctive. and if you go back and re-read and you think, oh, gosh, you know, 'what does he mean here? i want to ask a follow-up question' – send me a message and i'll be happy to answer it

and what were the other
events in 2016 that
had a big impact on
you? [*gasp*]
you should've given
me some notice for
that question! you
should've! I can't
    it's my last one,
it's fine. i'm going to
have to go soon. what
time's the train? 7.47?
7.49.
    it's fine. we've got
    you can talk for
another five minutes

Acknowledgements

This book is ultimately about people, and how great they are. I cannot thank all of my interviewees enough for their generosity and understanding. I hope I have done their stories justice in trying to bring them to the wider world. The advice of Theo Jones at the Society of Authors was also invaluable in helping me to navigate issues of copyright and licensing. My experience at the Oral History Summer School 2019 in Hudson, New York, was an inspiration. My thanks to Suzanne Snider and all the other participants for such an enriching time. Thanks also to Erin McKellar for her transcription expertise.

Special thanks are due to Professor Peter Jaeger and Professor Shelley Trower. To Sasha Dugdale, for her unwavering faith in the book.

My parents, for all their support. My partner, Padraig Reidy, thank you for all your love and understanding. And my daughter, Cora, thank you for turning up at just the right time.